Jailhouse Stories

Jailhouse Stories
Memories of a Small-Town Sheriff

Neil Haugerud

University of Minnesota Press
Minneapolis • London

Published by the University of Minnesota Press
111 Third Avenue South, Suite 290
Minneapolis, MN 55401-2520
http://www.upress.umn.edu

Library of Congress Cataloging-in-Publication Data
Haugerud, Neil.
    Jailhouse stories : memories of a small-town sheriff / Neil
Haugerud.
        p.   cm.
    ISBN 0-8166-3361-4 (alk. paper)
    1. Haugerud, Neil.   2. Sheriffs—Minnesota—Fillmore County
Biography.   I. Title.
HV7979.H38   1999
363.28′2′092—dc21
[B]   99-29882

Printed in the United States of America on acid-free paper

The University of Minnesota is an equal-opportunity educator and
employer.

11 10 09 08 07 06 05 04 03 02 01 00 99   10 9 8 7 6 5 4 3 2

Contents

*That so few now dare to be eccentric marks
the chief danger of the time.*

—John Stuart Mill

JAILHOUSE STORIES is my recollection of experiences associated with the sheriff's office in Fillmore County, Minnesota, in the mid-1950s and early 1960s. It is mostly about honorable, eccentric characters who happened to be alcoholics, just plain drunks, thieves, burglars, robbers, doctors, lawyers, judges, farmers, and ordinary citizens, if there is such a thing. I tend to believe not. I came to understand how people make a lot of mistakes, but in my view there are very few bad people.

Dr. Nehring, the county coroner, became such a rich source of unusual tales that I felt obliged to repeat them, first to my wife, Helen, then, after a small libation or two at social gatherings, to others. Thereafter on many occasions about town I'd be requested to tell Doc Nehring stories. My transition, from storytelling to story writing, late in life, after serving nine years in the Minnesota legislature and a stint with the federal government (where the cast of characters seems strikingly similar to that of my sheriff days), has been difficult and challenging. I first read one of my stories in public to the Minneapolis Writers Group in 1994. The group liked it and asked for more. With this as encouragement I began to search through the old jail register. The list of names jogged my memory of many people and incidents. I set about to weave the stories into a larger story of how they related to and affected our family life. We were one of the last sheriff families that served in an era when the family residence, the sheriff's office, and the jail were all in one building. In many ways we all became family. It is out of respect for these characters that I write. I hope you enjoy my interpretation of our experiences along this rather dusty path of life.

I thank the many people who gave direction for the writing of this book: Ashley Warlick, author of *Distance from the Heart of Things*, for setting me firmly on the path of reality and guiding me until I was able to walk by myself; Al Mathison and John Torgrimson of the *Fillmore County Journal* for believing in and publishing my column, "Jailhouse Stories"; the Minneapolis Writers Group for their listening and editorial critiques; and the Camp Creek Writers Club for their many lively discussions. And a thank you to my wife and daughters, who kept me from disposing of the manuscript in the fireplace on many occasions of self-doubt.

I had hardly flown all summer, that summer of 1958, and now it had passed, and there I was on the grass strip airfield at the Hammervold Farm and Flying Club, ready to get back in the air. I pulled our club plane, a vintage red-and-white two-seat Aeronca tail dragger, out of the hangar, checked the oil, and cleaned the beginning of a bird's nest from the engine cowling. With everything else ready to go, I chocked the wheels and gave the prop a spin. The engine sputtered, started at a gentle idle, and purred patiently while I removed the chocks. The air was still, the sky a clear, gorgeous fall blue. It was 7:45 A.M.

After takeoff, I made a left turn out of the flight pattern at four hundred feet and continued climbing, leveling off and throttling back to cruise speed at eight hundred feet, where I had a clear view of the country-side. I was born here in Fillmore County, named for Millard Fillmore, U.S. president in 1853, the year the county was incorporated. I was over Forestville, an abandoned town site in the Root River Valley, sur-rounded by nearly a thousand acres of dense hardwood forest. It was the business hub of the entire county until the railroad came through Preston, nine miles east. The Meighan family had owned the store and stables I flew over until they closed them in 1910, leaving everything—all the fixtures, dry goods, cold and sick-ness remedies, and sundry items—intact. They didn't remove an item, just locked up the store. Some folks propose to make the Forestville area a state park to preserve the rugged woodlands and make the store and village site a historical interpretive center. I smiled as I looked down at the crystal-clear river by the store building, where even today, more than fifty years later, in an unprotected rural setting, thieves had spared this historic treasure; nearly everything was still untouched. No wonder this county of twenty thousand people and 553,000 acres felt the need for only a sheriff and one deputy.

The landscape was pockmarked now with shallow, rusty, open-pit iron ore mines, some as small as an acre, others as large as ten. Many of the excavated areas had filled with water, providing habitat for snow geese and ducks. I could see them from the plane.

I neared another grass airstrip owned by a local mechanic named Bernard Peitenpol, who built his own airplanes with Model T Ford engines. From this height I could see the distinctiveness of the terrain, with its contrast between glaciated and nonglaciated land from the Ice Age. The ice had stopped here. To the west and south, flat open farmland; to the east, where I had come from, rugged hills and bluffs gouged by the glacier runoff. The hayfields and pastures, in this first part of November, held a dark green color, my favorite, the likes of which I had never seen elsewhere. During the previous week the hillsides, a match for any New England scene, had lost most of their glorious fall colors; only the stubborn brown-red leaves of the pin oaks and the burgundy leaves of the sumac gave contrast to the barren limbs in the woodlands.

I shot a few touch-and-go landings at Peitenpol Field to sharpen my skills. Throttle back, glide to the runway, stall out for a touchdown, then give full throttle for takeoff and go around for another. It was safer here than at Hammervold, which had a power line at one end of the runway and a deep gully at the other. No room for error there.

Touch and go, much like door-to-door campaigning, where you knock on the door, introduce yourself, ask strangers to consider you when they vote, and take off for the next house. I was running for sheriff of Fillmore County and I felt good about the campaign. I'd devoted practically my whole life to it since early June, and I thought I'd knocked on almost every door in the county. People had confidence in me and trusted my judgment, even though some thought that at twenty-eight I was too young for the job. I'd already served as deputy sheriff in the county for three years. Now, thank God, the campaign was over. All I had to do was cast my vote on Tuesday and wait till the wee hours of the morning for election results.

Flying broke me free of such concerns; it left the campaign on the ground behind me. When I was a kid I used to run downhill, with my arms extended, dipping from side to side, making airplane noises in simulated flight. Now with a mere nudge on the stick in the cockpit I could make it a graceful reality. I set the trim tab so I didn't even have to touch the controls and cruised back toward the town of Harmony, toward home. I could see a deer with two late fawns on the ground, chasing around a straw stack. I pulled the throttle back and glided in for a closer look.

One of the things about flying I like best is the quiet, serene glide without engine noise, only the rush of wind across the wings. My wife, Helen, never flew with me as pilot. She liked to have her feet on solid terra firma; she wouldn't go near the water or even climb past the third step of a stepladder. We set her on a little Shetland pony once and she screamed because it was too high for her.

So Helen hadn't come with me this morning; she was readying the children for church. I myself had Sunday school to teach, but there was still plenty of time. I planned to fly east and check out Roger Johnson's place. He'd asked if I'd give him a ride some day, and I knew on Sunday there was free time for farmers. Most of the people in Fillmore County were farmers, construction workers, truckers, or other tradespeople. I'd grown up on a family farm myself, one of ten children. I left the nest right after high school for a stint in the Marine Corps, knowing that gainful employment on the farm wasn't an option.

Even though Roger lived in a hilly area, I figured I could set the plane down in his hayfield without any trouble. I approached on a silent glide, then just above his house opened the throttle to announce my presence. The hayfield was on a hill, a level above the house with a long slope to the east. I buzzed it low and slow on the downhill run, looking for gopher mounds or woodchuck holes. Then I climbed, made my turn, and came back for a landing on the uphill slope. I didn't even have to apply the brakes. Takeoff downhill, without any wind, would be a piece of cake.

When I got to the house, Roger's wife, Alice, stood on the front steps.

"That was a fine way to wake up a household, Neil," she said.

"Is Rog home? I thought we could go for a spin."

"No, he went in to Harmony for something. What are you doing? I thought you were a Sunday school teacher."

"I've still got about an hour," I said.

"Is Helen going to be in church? I need to talk to her. I just found out our circle has to serve lunch at a funeral Tuesday. Lutherans and lunch. Lutherans and lunch. Sometimes I think they're the same word."

"Sure, we'll be there," I said.

I was looking forward to teaching my Sunday school class and going to church with my family. And maybe in the evening Helen and I could take in a movie for a change. She'd been on the campaign trail, too, although she was seven months pregnant and harbored a dislike for handing out campaign cards. "Like a door-to-door salesman," she'd said, and the way she said it, that was clearly not a good thing.

"Tell Rog we'll go flying another day," I told Alice.

I walked back up the hill and picked a Haralson apple off one of the trees before I climbed over the fence to the hayfield. The sun was warm and I unzipped my jacket. A red-tailed hawk circled peacefully above in the cloudless sky. *If things were going any better I'd have a runaway*, I thought.

With the plane facing uphill, I wouldn't need chocks. I turned on the key, did the preflight check, and gave the prop a spin. But even before I had time to step back, the plane was after me full throttle, growling and grabbing, trying to eat me up. I tripped over backward and the plane began to move. I rolled to the side to avoid the prop, jumped up, grabbed the wing strut with one hand, and opened the door with the other. With the plane picking up speed and turning downhill, I swung my feet up and tried to hook my ankles on the lower part of the doorway.

By now the plane was going faster than I could run. I either had to get in or let go of the strut. When it appeared my feet might leave the ground, I chose the latter and went tumbling and skidding head first across the hayfield. I watched in disbelief as the plane raced for the fence at the end of the field. *That'll be one hell of a crash when it hits that fence*, I thought.

To my amazement the damned thing lifted gracefully off the ground and cleared the fence like a breeze. *What the hell now?* I stood transfixed, staring, as if in a dream, wanting to wake up. *Fast.*

I watched the little plane climb out of the valley. About a mile away it began to turn to the right. Then I lost sight of it behind some hills. I spotted it again just above the horizon. It appeared to be making a wide circle that would bring it back to where I was standing. I waited. No, its path would bring it crashing into the barn. I shut my eyes.

When I didn't hear the crash, I opened them just in time to see the plane clear the barn roof by two feet. Then it roared past me just sixty feet in the air. I felt like my feet had sunk into the earth and my heart was beating below my navel. The damn thing began another circle that I calculated would bring it back near the vicinity of Roger and Alice's house.

The next thing I knew I was pounding on Alice's front door. I didn't even remember going over the fence. I let myself inside.

"Alice, Alice!" I shouted frantically. "Get the kids and get out of the house! The plane is coming!"

"Are you crazy, Neil? I just got out of the shower. I don't have any clothes on."

"Grab something. The plane got away from me and is heading for the house."

The urgency in my voice convinced her something was wrong, but she was too late. The plane cleared the house roof by ten feet before she arrived on the steps in her housecoat with the kids.

"You're trying to trick me," Alice said. "Who's the nut flying that thing?"

It took some lengthy explaining. Then the plane was making another circle, but it was getting higher so we were out of any immediate danger. I just stood helplessly watching it perform, while Alice and the kids got ready for church. It climbed in full one-mile circles, each carrying it farther southwest, toward Harmony.

I called Alice's brother-in-law, Dick Johnson. We'd hitch-hiked to the Dakotas together when we were sixteen to work the wheat harvest, and we'd been fast friends ever since. But we'd played a lot of tricks on each other, and I was having trouble making him believe this plane was not another joke, one I'd cooked up for his benefit. I couldn't get him to stop laughing.

"I'd a pissed my pants if that happened to me. Did you, Neil?" he chortled.

Alice dropped me off at his farm on the way to church. The plane was so high in the sky I could barely see it. Dick said he would drive and I should keep track of the plane. It was a picture of grace as it continued its climb, flying as if the most experienced pilot was at the controls. It was only a tiny speck high in the sky when we stopped at my home in Harmony.

Helen met us at the driveway. She was dressed in a navy blue maternity dress, with a white collar and buttons down the front. The baby was due the first week of January. She looked so pleasant and content with life. It was like breaking a spell. I didn't want to tell her what was happening.

She said, "What are you guys doing? Where's the car? I thought you were flying. What happened to your head and your jacket?"

I looked at my jacket, streaked with grass stains and dirt. My head was scraped up a bit from taking that dive in the hayfield. I realized I looked like I'd lost a few of my faculties, and Helen probably thought I'd crashed the plane or the car.

I pointed to the speck in the sky. "The plane is flying, but I'm not."

There was no time for explanation because suddenly the speck in the sky began a nosedive, seemingly aimed at the Lutheran church. I thought of my Sunday school class, waiting for my arrival beneath that steeple. I thought of my sister and her children, and all the others in danger if my plane crashed into it. I said a multitude of silent prayers and made a lot of promises to God I wouldn't be able to keep, if He would just help get that plane down without hurting anyone. And then the plane turned out of its dive and climbed just as steeply back into the air. It hung fluttering on its nose before it turned over for another dive. We all watched from the driveway as it repeated itself, each spiral bringing it closer to the earth.

I ran into the house and called the fire department. I told them to turn on the fire siren and keep it going until the plane crashed or flew away from town. Back in the driveway, we could hear the siren start its wailing, and I knew everyone in town would be thinking "fire," but at least many of the people would step outside to see where the fire engine might be going; that way if the plane came crashing their way, someone's life might be saved.

"Call the FAA," I shouted to Helen as Dick and I left the yard, as if she had any idea what or where the FAA was.

We drove with the car windows down. This was all my fault. Of course I could have called Roger before I left home and had him meet me at the airstrip. Or better yet, adhered to the advice of my instructor never to land anywhere other than at an authorized airfield, but that's no way to be a barnstormer; this wasn't the first time I had landed on a farm field. I was sure I had closed the throttle before I spun the prop, but was sure no one would believe it. I was having trouble believing it myself.

That Aeronca was wound up and screaming at such a pitch I thought the engine would come apart each time it pulled out of a dive. It pulled out of its next spiral a couple hundred feet above the church steeple. The next was near the west edge of town. One more and it would be clear of the city limits.

About this time, Dr. Hettig, a veterinarian, was driving back from a call. Doc Hettig and I had wet a line on occasion, in pursuit of wily trout, and sipped a spot or two of tea together. He screeched to a stop on the highway in front of us. It didn't appear that the plane would make another round. Now it was out over a harvested cornfield. It was pulling out of the dive when its wheels caught in the corn. The nose dipped down and the prop threw corn and dirt in the air trying to burrow a hole in the ground before the plane upended and cartwheeled, tearing the wings off.

Doc Hettig would say later that he had admired the ability of the pilot as he made his loops through the sky, before becoming upset that the pilot performed so close to town. Being a pilot himself, Doc said he damned near pulled the steering wheel off his car on the last turn. He remembered slamming on the brakes, pulling on the wheel, and yelling, "Pull her out! Pull her out!"

Then the crash came. "Look at that som-a-bitch come apart!" Dick shouted.

With the plane on the ground and no one injured and, miraculously, no other property damage, I gave thanks to God. Then, deranged excuse speeches for the voters began to flit through my brain. Brazen lies at first. "There was so much smoke in the cockpit I became disoriented, opened the door, and fell out." Or, "I'm suffering from sleep deprivation from the campaign and can't remember anything until I see the plane take off." I even thought of some kind of story with aliens launching the plane before taking me into their craft. But my conscious mind was so relieved I really didn't care about the election. The truth would suffice.

The crash site was a few hundred yards west of Dr. Wagner's house. I saw him leap the fence by his house carrying his black bag, his long legs churning toward the crash scene. Just two years ago Doc Wagner had delivered Susan, our second child.

Doc Wagner and a farmer were searching for bodies by the time I got to the scene. The doctor took a startled look at my head and jacket. "How the hell did you get out of there?" he asked.

"I wasn't in it," I said.

They started searching the cornfield again.

"There isn't a body in the plane. Whoever it was couldn't have been thrown far," the farmer said.

"There wasn't anybody in it," I said.

"What!?"

"There wasn't anyone in it."

"What!!"

"It got away from me when I started it."

Wag was speechless but only for a moment. "I can refer you to a good shrink, Neil," he said with a grin.

I still wasn't seeing the humor.

An hour later I lay on the floor of our living room, hyperventilating.

"I called the FAA," Helen said. "I'm sure they'll call back." I caught her implication that there'd be an investigation, and I detected a little smirk on her face, but she quickly turned away. I figured with the election just two days away this little fiasco would kick my chances of getting elected right square in the ass. Six months of gaining the confidence of people all shot to hell. *Not funny, Helen.*

Then the phone began to ring. United Press International . . . Associated Press . . . the *Minneapolis Tribune* . . . the *Rochester Post Bulletin* . . . ABC . . . CBS—it never quit. Monday's UPI headlines read, "Sheriff Candidate's Plane Takes 45-Minute 'Solo' Flight."

The next morning the phone began to ring again—school friends from throughout the nation, Marine Corps buddies from Louisiana.

"I don't know why you're messing with those newfangled gadgets," said one Cajun. "We both know your place is behind a plow."

With the election being held the next day, I was sure of it. I began to see the tragic humor of it all.

On Wednesday morning the phone rang yet again.

"Doc Wag here. Congratulations, Neil. You won handily. Damndest campaign stunt I ever heard of. I take coroner duty from time to time. Look forward to working with you. Stop by the office sometime after 5:30. We'll call a few friends, have a cup of prescription tea, and you can fill us all in on your strategies for getting elected to public office."

During the next weeks we put our house up for sale and made plans to move into the jailhouse. Traditionally, the sheriff and his family live in the jailhouse at Preston, the county seat. It's also traditional for the sheriff's wife to cook for and feed the prisoners, and we intended to carry on the tradition. Our family was big on tradition. After the election we enjoyed traditional Thanksgiving dinner, at noon, with my parents at their farmhouse near Harmony. Six of my nine brothers and sisters came, along with my aunt and uncle on my father's side. Ours was a rather emotionally cold family, and conversation with adults, other than my mother, was difficult at best.

We celebrated Christmas Eve at Helen's folks' home in Chatfield, twenty-five miles north of Harmony. A much different atmosphere there—open, friendly conversation flowed freely, and Helen's parents were totally indulgent toward the children, including me, and the grandchildren. Dinner at six: Norwegian meatballs and gravy, mashed potatoes, lefse, and lutefisk were the main fare, along with fattigmand, flatbread, rosettes, sand tarts, and pumpkin and apple pie. Our children Renee, three years old, and Susan, two, could hardly contain themselves through dinner in anticipation of opening the presents under the tree in the living room. Helen's two sisters, Mary Jo and Judy, were just as eager. My thoughts occasionally drifted to beginning my new position as sheriff, but I wasn't a bit anxious. I was twenty-nine; nothing much made me anxious.

Preparation for the move to the new living quarters proceeded without incident until the twenty-ninth of December, when Helen's blood pressure soared and her pulse raced at twice the normal rate. Dr. Wagner said there was a problem with the baby and referred her to the Lutheran hospital in La Crosse, Wisconsin. Our daughter Heidi was stillborn on the thirtieth. I spent the day with Helen and was at the hospital until after visiting hours on New Year's Eve.

The phone was ringing when I arrived home shortly after ten.

"Neil, this is Doc Nehring." Dr. Nehring was the county coroner. "Sheriff Link's wife died. I thought you should know." He filled me in on the details. She had been suffering from clinical depression, an illness that carried a social stigma and went mostly untreated in those days. She'd confided to a neighbor her fear of the future and said she would never leave the jailhouse. She took her own life.

My voice caught in the tightness of my throat and I struggled to respond to Doc.

"I'm so sorry" is all I managed to say. I knew her very well and had a close working relationship with her when I was the deputy sheriff. I felt guilt-ridden, thinking I was somewhat responsible by defeating her husband in the election.

I wasn't surprised that Dr. Nehring was blunt and to the point. I'd had many startling experiences with the doctor and had come to know him quite well during the time I was deputy sheriff, from 1954 until the summer of 1956. Doc had been practicing medicine in Preston since 1930, the year I was born. His father, Jesse Potter, died of typhoid fever in Belgrade, Minnesota, in December 1903. Doc was born on January 24, 1904. He took the name Jesse Potter Nehring at age ten when his mother remarried. My first official experience with Doc took place when I was twenty-four, a newly appointed deputy, embarking on my first investigation of a fatal auto accident.

In fatality cases, the sheriff's office and the coroner are required to conduct all official investigations of the death. I'd met the doctor semiprofessionally a few times, but didn't know him personally. When I called, Dr. Nehring said I should ride with him. He'd pick me up at my house.

As I waited on the porch, a frigid drizzle spiced the crisp, autumn air. I wore khaki trousers and a brown leather jacket over my plaid shirt; sheriffs and deputies didn't wear uniforms then. Doc pulled up in a green Plymouth sedan. When I got in, he was at the ready, with his hands on the steering wheel, humming a little tune that I later realized he always hummed when he was about to say something he thought profound.

Being young and inexperienced, and having mindfully placed doctors on a lofty perch, I waited for him to speak first. Five blocks took us to the edge of town. We crossed the railroad tracks by the feed mill with a noticeable bump.

Doc hummed his tune, "Hum te dum dum dum," and, as if it were a continuation of a sentence, asked, "How'd you like to make love to my wife, Neil?"

It was as clearly and simply stated as if he were asking the time of day.

This was the second sentence I'd heard from the man. Comprehension and response came slowly. His wife was kind of the grande dame of Preston, active in church circles and community, attractive, quiet, reserved, and polite. It occurred to me that a negative answer might be insulting, but an affirmative didn't seem appropriate either. I fumbled for a cigarette.

"I hadn't thought of that," I said. "Say, Doc, do you smoke? I left my smokes at the house."

"I quit smoking two years ago. Bad for your health."

We drove in silence for a time. I wondered if Doc asked

everybody about his wife, or if he maybe was setting me up for something. Doc hummed again.

"How'd you like to make love to Ole Swenson's wife?" He didn't wait for my answer. "Or Blacky Cobb's wife?" By the time we arrived at the accident scene he'd hummed his little tune twenty times and asked his question about at least that many women in town.

Nearly twenty onlookers were assembled at the scene when we began our official duties. The accident victim, on his way back from a fishing trip, had been thrown from the car, as had his minnow bucket, tackle box, and fishing poles. One of the coroner's duties is to inventory the personal property of the deceased. Doc found a half pack of cigarettes in the man's front overall pocket, soaked to mush in the cold rain and smeared with blood. He held them up for everyone to see and said, "Here, Haugerud, here's some cigarettes. You wanted a smoke, didn't you?"

I, too, was able to keep pretty much emotionally detached from the death scene, but wondered if, with time and experience, I'd become as callous about death as the doctor appeared to be. He acted as if he were center stage, and yet, as I observed closely, something about his mannerisms, tone of voice, and expressions didn't match his behavior. I thought it perhaps an act, a cover-up for a deeper sensitivity that he didn't want revealed. I would soon find that the more time I spent with the man, the more complex a person he seemed to be.

On the way home, Doc hummed a few more tunes. He talked mostly about money, which I learned later was another favorite subject.

Reflecting on past experiences, I knew that the greatest danger for me in being county sheriff was to become complacent and careless. Four years earlier, in 1954, the year Helen and I were married, I'd also run for sheriff and was narrowly defeated in the primary election.

Just prior to the general election that year, the county's only deputy sheriff was shot and killed while arresting a man for disturbing the peace, a man he'd known for years, who had never been in any serious trouble. Sheriff Link, who won the election, called and asked if I would be interested in filling the vacant deputy position. Helen was pregnant and I needed a job with benefits, so I didn't hesitate to accept.

I was cautious, even fearful at first, going out on calls with the sheriff. He was a seasoned officer, and to me it seemed he knew everyone in the county. My only experience had been occasionally pulling guard duty at the brig when I was in the Marine Corps. Our first arrest was an old rattlesnake hunter from Lanesboro who'd written a bum check. It was about 11 P.M.; Sheriff Link found our man in a Lanesboro tavern and put him in the front seat without frisking or hand-cuffing him. On the way to Preston, the sheriff drove, and the two of them talked like they were old pals while I sat in the back seat with my hand on an old .32 revolver I'd strapped to my belt. I was thinking, "This is the same kind of thing the deputy had been doing when he got killed."

During the next three years, Sheriff Link taught me many valuable lessons about law enforcement, but I also picked up a lot of careless habits, some by example and some on my own. Very seldom did either Sheriff Link or I handcuff a person we were bringing to jail, and we often responded to calls and made arrests alone. There's one lesson I'll never forget. The sheriff and I were bringing in Bart West, a rather mean and mouthy man. Sheriff Link was sitting up front with me; he'd handcuffed Bart and put him in the back seat. I hadn't driven far before I felt the chains between the handcuffs rake across my forehead, scrape down my nose, then jerk my Adam's apple to the back of my throat. It all happened in an instant, and I struggled to get one hand between the chain and my throat as Bart nearly pulled me into the back seat. I'll never know how I managed to stop the car or keep it from veering into oncoming traffic. Sheriff Link turned off the ignition, and together we were able to get the chain off my neck without serious injury. For the rest of the journey Sheriff Link sat behind me with Bart to his right. Even with that, the longer I served as deputy, the more I found myself being careless. I vowed to be more careful now that I was sheriff.

The county didn't provide patrol cars for the sheriff's department. Our family car was equipped with a two-way radio and two red lights installed above the bumper near the grill; it doubled as the official sheriff's vehicle. I also furnished a vehicle for the deputy sheriff. My first official call, on January 1, came from Lanesboro, a country town of nine hundred people, eight miles east of Preston. Corday Thompson, the town's only cop, called me at my home at 7:00 A.M. and reported that two gas stations had been burglarized.

I had first met Corday, a fifty-nine-year-old rugged-looking Norwegian, when he caught me and several of my friends tipping over outhouses on Halloween during my junior year in high school. He'd taken our names and supervised while we put the structures back in place. Then he showed us what the inside of the town lockup looked like before he sent us home. Corday had reminded me of this incident several times while I was deputy.

Now he met me at the Shell station. The door had been forced open and several tires had been taken, along with shotgun shells and .22 caliber rifle ammunition. We went across the street to the Standard station. In both stations the cigarette and candy machines had been broken into and the money stolen, along with most of the cigarettes. Corday and I went through the usual procedures of looking for evidence and dusting for fingerprints.

"Whoever did this wasn't satisfied with just breaking in and carrying off the loot," I said. "He had to make a mess, bang up things, and scatter everything around he didn't intend to steal, like Orlin Epson used to."

"You don't need to worry about Orlin anymore, Neil," Corday said.

"Why?" I asked.

"He's twenty-one now and moved to the Cities. He's a shirttail relative of mine, you know. I talked to him last summer, he's got a good job. Told me he has straightened right out."

"That's good," I said, but inside my gut feeling told me this was too much like the kind of mess I'd seen when Orlin was a juvenile on a burglary spree.

"His folks still live in Rushford?" I asked casually.

"Whose?"

"Orlin's."

"Ya, over in south Rushford."

"We don't have anything else to go on at this point. Let's take a ride down that way and see if Orlin has been around. It's only twenty miles."

"Okay by me, but it's a wild goose chase."

Corday knew right where the Epson house was. A Chevrolet four-door was parked outside. I could tell it wasn't a local car—it had a coat of soot on it, which you don't get parking your car in small towns. I figured it was more than likely from the Twin Cities. The soot on the top of the trunk door was messed about.

"I'd like to get a look in that trunk," I said to Corday.

"I thought I saw that car in Lanesboro last night but I didn't know whose it was," Corday said. We went to the house and knocked on the door. Orlin's mother, a pale woman with stringy, uncombed hair, came to the door wearing a housecoat. She grimaced; she apparently recognized me from past experience when I was a deputy.

"Is Orlin home?" I asked.

She turned to look at Corday. "What's going on, Corday?" Corday looked down, shuffled his feet a bit, and nodded toward me.

"We'd like to talk to Orlin if he's home," I said.

She stood to the side of the door and motioned us in. Her husband sat at the kitchen table drinking coffee and smoking a cigarette.

"They're asking about Orlin," she said.

"Ya, I heard. He's upstairs in bed," the husband said. "What's the problem?"

"Anyone with him?" I asked.

"They came in late. I don't know. Everett Nyland was with him yesterday."

I knew Everett, too. He was another young burglar I'd had a previous acquaintance with.

"There were two burglaries in Lanesboro last night. Just a couple of questions and I'm sure we'll have this cleared up and we'll be on our way. That his car outside?" I asked.

"Yeah, but Orlin doesn't do stuff like that anymore," the husband said. "I'll have him come down."

When Orlin came down, one look at him was enough for me. He sized up our position and glanced toward every possible exit looking for a way out.

"Hey, Orlin," I said pleasantly. "Haven't seen you for a few years."

"Why are you always after me? I haven't done anything," Orlin grumbled coarsely.

"I don't want to cause you any trouble, Orlin. Just give me a quick peek in the trunk of your car. After that I'll say I'm sorry to have bothered you and be on my way."

"No way, you don't have any right. Where's your search warrant? Got a search warrant?"

"No, but I expect I can get one, and we can have your car impounded until we do."

Orlin's parents glared at their son.

"Oh, no!" his father exclaimed.

"Shut up, Dad," Orlin said. "I want a lawyer." Everett came downstairs. I informed Orlin and Everett that I was taking them into custody for investigation. Orlin called a local attorney, who arrived on the scene fifteen minutes later. He wasn't exactly an expert in criminal law.

"Here's the situation," I said. "Orlin's car was seen in the vicinity of a burglary; he's got a previous record. We picked up fingerprints at the scene. It's obvious to us someone has recently opened the trunk. We intend to impound the car until we get a search warrant. By then we will have compared the prints." It was a total bluff—a tough one to pull off.

After further discussion, Orlin was convinced that at some point I was legally going to get the trunk of his car open and the attorney didn't say otherwise. Orlin threw the keys to the attorney.

"Open it up, then," he said. I told Orlin and Everett to sit down in the kitchen chairs, while Corday went with the attorney to open the trunk. The shotgun shells, tires, and coin boxes from the cigarette machines were inside. When Corday came back into the house we handcuffed the boys together and frisked them.

Corday and the attorney inventoried the stolen property and placed it in the trunk of my car while I kept watch over Orlin and Everett. Then Corday and I put them in the back seat and we proceeded to Preston. Four hours after my first official call, two burglaries, the property was recovered and the burglars were in jail. I began to feel better about my ability, which I'd been questioning since the airplane incident. I was concerned about Corday feeling a bit disenfranchised, so when the *Rochester Post Bulletin* called that afternoon I began my story with, "Acting on a tip from Lanesboro's Chief Thompson . . ."

It was after six that night by the time I'd written out the confessions of Orlin and Everett and after seven by the time I'd driven the sixty miles to the hospital to visit Helen; I'd called and talked to her several times during the day. She'd fixed her hair, applied a small amount of makeup, as she usually did, and was propped up in bed. She wanted to talk about the baby; emotionally it was a great loss for her, something I didn't fully understand at the time.

"She's got to have a name," Helen said. "We talked about Heidi before; I'd like that."

"That's fine with me." I was surprised by how detached I felt and how different it was for Helen. Her parents had been there earlier in the day and brought flowers and a card. I'd come empty-handed, something traditional in my family.

Then I told her about the death of Sheriff Link's wife. Helen just closed her eyes and shook her head; I put my arms around her and we didn't speak further of it that evening. New Year's Day was drawing to a close before I left the hospital. I was physically and mentally drained.

It wasn't until early February that we were able to move into our living quarters at the jail. In consideration of Sheriff Link's family tragedy, we allowed him to take his time getting his things in order. He continued to feed the prisoners, answer the phones, and refer the calls to me at home at night.

The jailhouse, an unimposing, two-story brick building, was situated on a tree-lined residential street in the town of Preston, nestled deep in the Root River Valley of central Fillmore County. The jailhouse included the county jail, the sheriff's office, and a residence for the sheriff and his family. There was a triple garage and expansive yard in back, encompassing a quarter block in all. The front of the building faced east, appearing more like a house or duplex than a jailhouse. Across the north street was a quaint white wood-frame Lutheran church with small stained-glass windows and a sharp, high steeple. A stately Catholic church and parson-age of brick were located one block west. Otherwise we were surrounded by modest family dwellings.

Moving day was hectic but rather festive. I enlisted the aid of my brother and two farmer friends to help. I kept getting office calls, which prevented me from actively taking part in the move, and I was severely chided by my helpers. I found time, however, to help carry all the bedroom furniture up the open stairway to the second floor, where there were five large bedrooms, high-ceilinged and airy; two had walk-in closets. The walls were papered with what I thought of as generic, old-fashioned wall-paper with little flowers. And in the middle of the long hall, off to the right, was a spacious bathroom with a huge old-fashioned claw-footed bathtub. Another short stairway at the north end of the hall descended to a landing and led through a doorway to the main jail door. All the floors were covered with linoleum. The linoleum in our bedroom had been painted over and nearly drove Helen nuts during the next few months, with its chipping and sticking to our feet and even finding its way into our bed. Renee and Susan wanted the bedroom directly across the hall from Mom and Dad's room. They scurried about the living quarters, unaware that this was any different from the home we had moved from. The sheriff's office was much like another room of the home. Its south door opened into our large kitchen. The kitchen walls were a light yellow with white woodwork trim; on the south wall were two seven-foot windows. Helen made coffee and rummaged through the boxes until she found the moving crew something for lunch. Then she discovered that the treasured doll bed her grandfather had made for her was missing. We looked in all the boxes and drove back to our old house, with the kids looking all along the highway as we drove, without luck. This loss was magnified in significance for Helen in light of all the misfortunes we'd faced lately. It was nearly five o'clock when our helpers left and we sat down at the kitchen table for a rest.

But not for long. It was time to feed the prisoners—five of them. There was a dumbwaiter in the northwest corner of the kitchen. It looked like an ordinary cupboard from the outside; inside were wooden shelves, painted gunmetal gray, and a rope-and-pulley mechanism to lift the shelves to the jail. We only had to raise the shelves about two feet for the prisoners on the first floor to get their food.

"What am I going to feed those guys?" Helen asked. The phone rang in the office before I could respond.

"Sparky Bartlett is on a rampage," I said to Helen when I returned to the kitchen. "I'll have to go up and get him."

Sparky was a livestock jockey who lived on a little farm on the outskirts of Spring Valley, eighteen miles to our west. Helen had first met Sparky several years before, when I was a deputy. We'd been driving to church in a gentle rain when the sheriff called on the radio.

"Office to car 2."

"Car 2, go ahead," I replied. Helen frowned; she figured our Sunday outing was going to be disrupted. In Fillmore County, any time a deputy could be located by telephone or radio he was on duty.

"The Spring Valley P.D. called. Sparky ran off the road just south of town. Can you go get him?" the sheriff asked.

"Okay, I'll take care of it," I said.

"Ten-four."

"Want to ride along, Helen?" I asked. The kids had stayed overnight with her parents.

"Who's Sparky? Maybe I should go home."

"Oh, just kind of a harmless guy who goes on a month-long binge once in a while. Normally he hires a driver before he gets started. On his last binge he went to Montana for three weeks; he had a driver with him all the time. He eventually got thrown in jail out there. The driver waited in a hotel four days for him to get out. He's always broke by the time the binge is over."

"You're sure it's safe for me to go along?" Helen asked.

"I'll put him in the back seat; you'll be all right," I replied. By now we were on the highway to Spring Valley.

"Okay," Helen said. "It appears I'm going, regardless."

I chuckled and told Helen the story of the time the sheriff brought Sparky down from jail to answer phones and handle the radio while he and I went on an emergency call. Sparky was dead broke; he'd even had his pickup repossessed. When we returned from our call, Sparky was in the office with his feet up on the desk, talking on the phone to his former hired man.

"Take the stuffed owl off the piano and take it over to old man Wister's place and trade it for as many guinea hens as he'll give for it. Take the guinea hens over to Lester Hare's place and trade them for a sucking calf. Take the sucking calf to Elmer Ott's and get ten feeder pigs. Take the feeder pigs to Skinny Eisner's and get a check for a hundred dollars. You got that straight?"

The jail keys were in my hand, ready to take Sparky back to jail.

"Just a minute," he said. "I got one more call to make."

He dialed the phone.

"Skinny, I got ten nice feeder pigs I'll let you have for a hundred bucks," he said.

The hired man came to visit Sparky for instructions, and two days later, when Sparky was released, they'd bartered for a used pickup, bought the stuffed owl back, and purchased a box of White Owl cigars. Sparky was back in business.

It was raining steadily when Helen and I got to Spring Valley. We first saw Sparky, wearing a tan suit coat over a pair of striped bib overalls, lurching along the highway south of town; then he slipped and fell. Covered with mud from head to foot, he was climbing out of the ditch on all fours as I pulled to the side of the road. Before I could get to him, all two hundred and thirty pounds of him, he got to the side of my car, opened the door, and tumbled in on top of little Helen. By the time she escaped from underneath him, her new spring outfit looked as if she'd been stumbling in the mud and rain with Sparky. Sparky drooled something the color of split pea soup onto the front of Helen's white blouse and blubbered something that I took as "Didn't see you there, Mrs." Helen managed to slide out the driver's side door, got into the back seat, and locked the doors.

With such an introduction, Sparky was a hard man to forget.

"You better take someone with you," Helen said, and I caught a hint of the daggers she'd had in her eyes for me that day long ago.

"I'll be okay," I said. "Leave the kitchen door to the office open so you can hear me on the radio if I need anything."

I wondered how Helen was feeling about her first day at our new house. Earlier we'd talked about Heidi. Helen's side of the family was very emotional and sentimental, observing everyone's birthdays with a celebration, cakes, presents, and cards. My side of the family hardly made notice of birthdays while we were growing up and often forgot them entirely. Helen lived at home with her parents before we were married and taught in a one-room country school. She'd gone to Normal Teacher Training School in Austin, Minnesota, for one year to get her teaching degree. She and her two sisters were very close. Among my five sisters and four brothers, none of us, as yet, had learned to talk to each other—or to our parents, for that matter. It bothered me that I wasn't bothered about Heidi the way Helen was. I thought of Helen alone there at the jail with two young children, cooking for five prisoners, listening for the two-way radio, and answering the office phone. I wondered if this was the kind of life she wanted, if I was the kind of man she wanted. Maybe baby-sitting a jailhouse full of misfits at suppertime was too much to ask.

Sparky wasn't too bad when I picked him up, although he'd been ingesting that green stuff with the awful odor again. Halfway to Preston, he reached in his pocket, pulled out a wad of money, and handed it to me.

"Saay, Sheriff," he said, "when we get to Preston, stop and get me a box of White Owls."

Sparky was a wet-lipped cigar smoker. Even sober he always licked his lips wet, rolling his cigar around in his jowls like a pig with a stick. A few miles further he pulled another wad of bills out of another pocket.

"Saay, Sheriff," he repeated, "get me a box of White Owls when we get to Preston."

By the time we arrived at the jail, Sparky had handed me more than a hundred dollars in wadded-up bills and made his request a half dozen times. I inventoried all of his personal property and put him in a cell for the night.

Renee and Susan were upstairs in bed by the time I had finished with Sparky, but they were still awake. Helen had been telling them bedtime stories, and they were waiting for me to give them a poink. I'd hold each of them, one at a time, in a level position, face up, about four feet above her bed and then let go. We'd say "poink" when she bounced on the bed. That was the beginning of the balancing act: Helen and I both living two separate lives under this same roof, with our roles often changing, sometimes from minute to minute.

The next morning, I let Sparky out of his cell into the main compound for breakfast.

"Say, Neil, did I have any money on me when you brought me in last night?"

"Ya, some, Sparky."

"You wouldn't get me a box of White Owls when you go downtown, would ya?"

Irvin—My Friend

The jail register, a bulky, seventeen-inch-square, leather-bound book turning maroon with age, was kept on the counter in the sheriff's office. On the first page, dated December 20, 1948, was the name Irvin Johnson. He'd served eighteen days for being drunk and again on January 28 was jailed for the same offense. His name appeared frequently in the register every year thereafter.

I first booked Irvin on December 20, 1954. Offense: drunk. He was fifty-two, a smooth-featured six-foot-tall man, who, even when he was drinking, was mild-mannered and spoke with a decidedly Norwegian accent. During the next thirteen years I came to know Irvin very well.

Possibly the worst shape Irvin Johnson was in, other than the way he died, was in the heat of late July 1960, when he'd holed up with a stash of beer and booze in an outhouse behind the railroad depot in Canton. On the twelfth day of his binge, when I was called to bring him in, he was wet, pickled, and ripe. He could stand if I held him up or leaned him against a wall, but he couldn't walk without help. I knew a sage old man once, himself quite familiar with the sauce, who told me, "You've never really been drunk till you shit your pants." Well, Irvin was drunk. He'd also been drinking paraldehyde, whose nearly paralyzing aroma was more offensive than anything produced by his not using the toilet facility for three or four days. Paraldehyde is a sort of hypnotic sedative that allowed Irvin to continue drinking when he was too sick to drink anymore. A doctor prescribed it for Irvin to enable him to stop drinking, but he used it to continue. I felt that a small whiff of paraldehyde could cauterize a nose bleed.

On another occasion, Irvin broke into the liquor store at Mabel and scribbled a note while he was there. It read, "Neil, I just had to have a shot of whiskey." I prevailed upon the city fathers to let Irvin fix the door and do some painting and carpentry work for them after he was sober rather than file charges. Irvin wasn't a burglar. He was a drunk. He'd been to the jag farm five times without any positive results, so now when he was brought in Doc Nehring would attend to him and administer vitamin B shots until he recovered. He'd be kept in jail for at least forty-five days or he'd be back, sick and drunk, two days after we let him out. After about ten recovery days in jail, he was ready to become our trusted handyman, mowing the lawn, washing storm windows, painting, fixing cupboards, doing errands for Helen, and helping out the neighbors. Renee and Susan, who were not allowed to cross the street alone, enlisted him to walk across the street with them so they could play with their friends.

"You're such a nice man, Irvin," Renee said, holding his hand as they walked. "How come you're in jail?"

"I've been a bad boy," Irvin said.

In the early sixties, heavy drinking, fighting, brawling, and the Green Gables, a so-called night club at Fountain, were nearly synonymous terms. Especially during the "festive season," a season that began after harvest in November and continued until its culmination on New Year's Eve. One festive season I was called to quell a brawl at the Gables. I had six combatants in my station wagon and my deputy standing guard over three more. On this occasion a group of cattlemen (we weren't far enough out west for them to be called cowboys) had wound up their day of pregnancy testing cows and castrating calves, whereupon they exchanged a few pulls off a bottle of peppermint schnapps and decided to go directly to the Gables, taking a pail of testicles with them.

"We can get old Ray to fry us up a bunch of these oysters," one of them said.

Ray was frying the oysters and the cattlemen had quaffed a number of beers when a group of off-duty Ruan petroleum transport drivers, enjoying the festive season with several of their girlfriends, arrived on the scene. They took some offense to the odor the cattlemen had brought with them and politely asked them to leave.

"How about you stinking cowshit farmers getting the f—— out of here," was the way it was put.

When the deputy and I first pulled up and parked

outside near the gas pumps, we observed through the barroom window several gentlemen engaging in fisticuffs. Thankfully, there was great respect for the law, especially the sheriff's department, during those times. I thought nothing of stepping between two ruffians throwing punches at each other. I didn't have to lay a hand on them, just ordered them to stop.

"But Goddamn it, Sheriff," was the first response. The next step was to quiet the ensuing arguments, a more difficult task. During several attempts at quashing the disturbance I placed six of the most obstinate and inebriated of the bunch outside in my car. I had just gotten them quieted when I glanced up and saw another fight break out in the barroom. I had to bring out two more participants of the fray to join the group outside and admonished the rest of the crowd that any further disturbance by anyone would result in an immediate trip to jail.

After getting the names and addresses of the individuals outside, I gave all but four of them a choice of a peaceable trip home or a peaceable trip with me to the county jail. Upon agreement, I spaced their willing departures five minutes apart. The remaining four celebrants were too drunk to drive and too mean to let go, so they spent the night in "Haugerud's Hotel."

We had several more calls to similar social clubs in the county during the remainder of the festive season.

The following June I had another memorable call to the Gables. This time Pat O'Grady was on the ground choking his distant relative Ben O'Grady when I arrived. Pat's son Wilbur, a former Golden Glove boxer, had raised a fair-sized shanty on Lyle Connor's eye while warding off his attempt to intervene on his friend Ben's behalf.

With a few strong words and a tug on his shoulder I persuaded Pat to quit throttling his cousin, then saw to it that Ben was getting air and would survive.

It was Saturday night and I knew I wouldn't get any rest all weekend if I hauled these two O'Gradys off to jail with me. So I took them aside and got their promise to go home and stay until I came to see them on Monday morning.

Pat and Wilbur lived and farmed within a mile of the night club, and I wasn't sure I could trust them to stay home once they got there.

"Well, Sheriff, you have me sacred word on me fine mither's name," Pat drawled in his coarse Irish brogue. Wilbur, docile and subservient to his father, nodded agreement.

Lyle Connor and his wife paid me a visit on Sunday morning and had some choice words with me for not locking Pat and Wilbur up on Saturday night. I told them a sheriff's job wasn't to punish, but to keep the peace. I said it was a lot easier to stop fights if you had a reputation for being considerate. The courts were responsible for meting out judgment and punishment, and I would have Pat and Wilbur before the court on Monday. They didn't like it, but that's the way it was.

Big, rawboned Pat O'Grady, as gregarious as any Irishman with the gift can be, greeted me at his door on Monday morning.

"Sheriff, Sheriff!" he said, as if surprised to see me. "Come right in, Sheriff. Mother has coffee on."

They lived in a fairly new two-story white frame farmhouse in a pastoral setting near the highway. Wilbur, as rugged-looking as his father, stood shyly just inside the door by an open stairway, which I assumed went to the basement, but it was filled to the brim with household garbage—milk cartons, cereal boxes, plastic bags, tin cans, and beer bottles. Pat ushered me quickly to the kitchen table, along a path through discarded household items on the floor.

"Sit right down, Sheriff," he said.

Nodding to his wife, a woman with a full head of auburn hair in bad need of combing, he said, "Mother! Pour the sheriff some coffee." Then, turning to me, he asked, "Cream or sugar, Sheriff?" His wife turned from the stove and brought coffee in a blue speckled enamel coffee pot. Her shoulders were as wide as her husband's. She was nearly as tall as he and had a begrudging look on her face, which led me to believe my presence wasn't exactly appreciated.

"Yes, a bit of cream," I said pleasantly. An open box of corn-flakes and breakfast bowls sat atop the blue-and-white oilcloth covering the table. I stirred in the cream and sipped my coffee.

"I have warrants for your arrest," I said to Pat and Wilbur.

"Ah, yes, a terrible misunderstanding, I'm sure," Pat replied. "I'm sure we can explain. Who do we appear before, Sheriff?"

"Judge Murray."

"Yes, yes, a fine Catholic man, Judge Murray, and county attorney Herrick, too."

Wilbur only smiled. I took a little time to finish my coffee while Pat continued with his blarney.

"We'd better be on our way," I said after a bit.

"Well, Sheriff, you know Wilbur and I are fine American citizens. Why don't we just drive down to court by ourselves and that will save you the trouble of driving us back. Why'n't you just follow us down to Preston? Wilbur here will drive our car."

"That'll be fine," I said.

I went to my car and waited while they changed. Soon Pat and Wilbur came from the house, both wearing dark wool serge suits in need of pressing and brown felt hats with the front brims turned down.

I first thought the screen door on the house must have exploded as Pat and Wilbur started down the drive in their car. Then I saw flailing arms and legs attached to a head of unmanageable hair burst through the doorway, and "Mother" rushed to the car and thrust herself into the back seat. A very animated conversation between Mother and Pat ensued for several minutes while the car idled at the end of the drive. Pat alighted from his passenger seat, strolled back to my car, and opened the door.

"Saaay, Sheriff," he said. "Would you mind at all if I rode down to Preston with you? It seems Mother is a little bit disturbed." Pat and I followed as Wilbur and "Mother" drove to the courthouse in Preston.

At court Pat and Wilbur were found guilty of disturbing the peace, and each was fined one hundred dollars. After being told by Pat what marvelous citizens, responsible public servants, and fine Catholic men they were, the judge and the county attorney, with big smiles on their faces, agreed to Pat's request to suspend fifty dollars of each fine.

"Say, Sheriff," Pat said. "Do you suppose I could hitch a ride home with you, too? I think Mother needs a bit more time to herself." I gave Pat a ride home, knowing more than likely there would be a "next time" with the O'Gradys.

We drove hurriedly, Doc Nehring and I. I turned the heater up for warmth on that eighteen-degree mid-December night.

"I hope we get some snow before Christmas," Doc said. I'd picked him up at his house a few minutes earlier. Our headlights searched across the brown grassy ditches and directed us around the sharp curves of the narrow gravel road. The heater fan droned and Doc closed his eyes. He looked weary and was unusually quiet. He hadn't even said, "What do you think of me, Neil? Am I a pretty good guy?" as he often did when he got in the car with me. I'd recently learned that Doc had worked his way through med school in speakeasies, playing saxophone and clarinet with his own five-piece band during the late twenties. This helped explain his incessant humming.

We passed over a narrow bridge, and after a few more dusty miles I made out the taillights of several cars parked on a steep hill ahead. The red light from the police bubble on top of my car flashed across the scene, through bare treetops rising from a steep gully.

"There's a woman down at the bottom of the embankment!" a man shouted as we came to a stop and Doc got out. I turned the car around and parked where my searchlight could illuminate the gully. A hundred feet down through brush and woods a car was wrapped around a tree. Doc and I held on to heavy brush to keep our balance on the way down the steep incline. Guided by my flashlight, we proceeded past another tree, scarred by the wreck, and I helped Doc slide down on his rear the last few feet to a gravel draw. The reflection of the flashing red light and the beam of white from the spotlight brightened the brushy area. A husky woman's voice came from a distance.

"Oh, oh, *Rescue Eight, Rescue Eight*," she said. "This is just like *Rescue Eight.*" The flashlight and the sound of her voice directed us to her. I shone the light her way. She'd been thrown from the wreck and was lying in a pile of bloody leaves. She wasn't wearing a coat and her print housedress and light sweater were splotched with blood.

"*Rescue Eight*," she kept repeating. This was the name of a popular TV show about emergency rescue missions.

"Alma!" Doc exclaimed as he went to her side and knelt down. "Where do you hurt, Alma?"

"Don't know, Doc," she said. "I can't move anything but my mouth." Doc checked her over. The ambulance and crew (the hearse, the funeral director, and his sidekick) arrived on the scene. Alma was paralyzed from the neck down. Doc had determined that, with help from the cold weather, Alma's serious bleeding had stopped.

"What happened, Alma?" Doc asked.

"We were up in Fountain to see Santa Claus. It's Santa Claus day in Fountain today, Doc," Alma responded, her voice thick and lively.

"Where was Santa?" Doc questioned.

"The liquor store. Where do you suppose, you dumb shit, Doc." Doc chuckled.

"You know Alma here, don't you, Neil?" he said.

"I think so. I know I've seen her around," I said.

"Hell yes, you know me, Neil," Alma said.

Cautiously, after the ambulance crew brought a stretcher, we carried her a half mile down the draw to where we could get back to the road more easily. The freezing temperature didn't seem to bother Alma at all. It bothered me.

"*Rescue Eight*, just like *Rescue Eight*," Alma repeated as we placed her in the ambulance for the trip to Emergency at Saint Mary's Hospital in Rochester.

"Alma comes from a long line of tough stock. She was a Corwin girl," Doc said.

I'd heard it said that on the day Alma was born, her mother was cultivating corn. She tied the team to the fence, went in the house, had the baby, and was back in the field in two hours. Later, when the team needed a rest, she went to the house to nurse Alma.

The next day we learned that Alma had a broken neck. Six months later she was on her way to a full recovery.

"Only a Corwin girl could make a recovery like that," Doc said.

I saw Alma just the other day. She's in her mid-eighties now and lives independently in her own home. She was trotting into the nursing home, where she volunteers with the residents, many of whom are younger than she.

She's a Corwin girl, you know.

Three mature walnut trees stood by the jail, two out front and one on the south side. A genuine old hoot owl lived in one of the trees, I'm not sure which. As days went, my day as sheriff had been relatively uneventful. We boarded nine prisoners: three drunks, a check forger, a mental patient awaiting hearing, and four small-time burglars, two of whom had previously broken jail. The burglars were locked in the upstairs bull pen. We had two bull pens, one on each floor. They were very secure lockups, with heavy steel bars located six feet from any exterior walls. Each had four separate cells, two bunks to a cell.

Renee, now seven years old, and Susan, five, wanted to sleep outside. I pitched a small tent for them near the walnut tree on the south side of the jail, and we retired at 9:30. Of course, I had to sleep out with them. The hoot owl started in about eleven o'clock. "Whoo-whoo-who-who. Who cooks for you? Who cooks for you?" I calmed the girls down and convinced them we could survive the night, and soon they fell asleep. I was drifting off to sleep myself when a fearful commotion erupted from the jail, followed by a frightful scream, which was throttled to a gurgle partway through. The girls levitated to their feet and covers flew.

"Dad, Dad! What was that?" they shouted, eyes so wide they put the owl to shame.

"Something's going on in the jail. You better go inside. Wake Mom," I said. I thought the disturbance had erupted from the upstairs bull pen.

"Help! Help! Help!" someone howled from above.

It's quite bizarre, the unexpected situations a rural sheriff running a county jail gets into. There was no time to second-guess myself. I had to act quickly, instinctively, without hope of assistance. I was fairly sure, but I needed to question whether this was a real emergency or whether I was being suckered into the jail by some desperate inmates. I ran inside, realizing I'd be putting myself at risk, and plucked the jail keys from my desk drawer, dreading the idea of locking myself inside the jail without backup support. The shouting from above continued as I clambered up the metal stairs, two at a time, to the bull pen.

Inside the bull pen, Johnny Karl was choking his cell mate. Two other inmates were attempting to pry Johnny's hands loose from his victim's throat. I couldn't take the chance on being suckered—the guy's face was turning purple. I unlocked the door and went in. We all struggled mightily to unlock Johnny's fingers from the man's windpipe. Finally succeeding, we wrestled Johnny to the cement floor. He was a strapping twenty-one-year-old possessing near superhuman strength, and he had gone totally berserk. It took all of us to keep him subdued until one of the drunks from downstairs, now sober, came to help. They held Johnny down while I went to call Doc Nehring. I also called Dale Thauwald for an ambulance. Doc Nehring, always prompt, met me at my office in less than ten minutes. "What have you got, Neil?" he asked.

"Prisoner's gone berserk, Doc," I said. "You got anything to knock him out so we can get him up to Rochester on an emergency commitment?"

"Sure, lead me to him." Doc fumbled through his black bag and brought out a vial and a hypodermic syringe.

Inside the main jail door, Doc sort of grunted and gave me an uncomfortable look as the solid steel door clanged behind him. I locked us in and dropped the heavy ring of keys in my pocket and proceeded upstairs. Doc didn't care for the commotion inside the bull pen and stopped short of the door.

"I'll stay out here, Neil. Let me know when you got him ready."

Johnny was thrashing around on his stomach and with the back of his arm easily lifted the hundred-and-fifty-pound man trying to subdue him off the floor. I secured one of Johnny's arms the best I could.

"Okay, Doc, hurry up," I said.

Doc darted in, hurriedly administered the shot, and darted out again.

"Goddamn it, Doc!" exclaimed one of the prisoners assisting us. "That was *my* arm!" Doc searched through his bag for another vial. The injected prisoner began to drift off.

"I've got his arm, Doc," I said. "Now take your time and get the right one this time. I'm needed around here." Doc peered around the corner at me.

"Sure you got him, Neil?"

"Yes, get the hell in here!" I was growing somewhat agitated. "I think Dale is knocking on the door downstairs."

It took two of Doc's shots to get Johnny subdued. Then, when Dale arrived, we tied Johnny to a stretcher with belts and towels before loading him into Dale's duel-purpose ambulance-hearse.

Dale, a middle-aged gray-haired man, adopted the stereotypical look of an undertaker when on official business. He reminded me of some old-time ministers I'd known whose faces tended to mimic the corpse at funerals. But to a keen observer Dale had the mischievous look of the devil in his eye. He was one of our poker-playing cronies, a character of considerable dry humor. He and I spent a good number of times winding Doc up over the years. When engaging in trickery, Dale, I noticed, always pursed his lips and lightened his voice a bit.

On the way to Rochester, I sat in the back of the hearse with the prisoner, and Doc sat in the front seat with Dale. A sliding window panel opened between us, allowing us to converse. On the outskirts of Rochester, Dale pursed his lips, turned to me, and pointed to a motel alongside the road.

"That's a good short-time motel, Neil." I detected Dale's impishness and knew he was up to something for Doc's edification.

"Thanks, Dale," I said, acting only half interested. "I'll keep that in mind if the need arises." Doc twisted his neck, turning first to me, then to Dale, and asked, "Whaddaya mean, Dale, short time?" I saw Dale's eyes twinkle in the rearview mirror.

"You know, Doc," Dale said. "If you got this bim and you need a room. You don't want to pay for the whole night, do you?"

"Oh," Doc said.

We arrived at the state hospital just past midnight, our patient resting comfortably. Doc walked with me to the administration building while Dale stayed in the ambulance. Rochester's hospitals are famous for employing foreign interns. That night a six-foot, steely-eyed young German intern with a crew cut greeted us. I explained how I was the county sheriff and we had an emergency commitment.

"This is Dr. Nehring, our county medical officer," I said. The intern turned from me to confer with his professional equal; he stood straight arrow at attention, military style, and in my mind's eye I'd have sworn he clicked his heels.

"Vot are de symptoms, Dok-tor?" he asked. His official-sounding sharp tones left a ringing noise in the room. Doc Nehring paused and blinked once; his grapelike eyes seemed to moisten as he looked the intern over slowly.

"The son-of-a-bitch is nuts," Doc said. "Where's the papers to sign?" The intern jumped backward a couple of hops, the heels of his shoes clicking on the terrazzo floor while his aura of official-dom came apart about him. No one could deflate pretension like Doc Nehring.

Doc insisted on treating us to hamburgers at an all-night joint before leaving Rochester. Then we shared a quiet ride home. Back at the jail, Doc, who had apparently been thinking about something all the way from Rochester, stepped out of the ambulance and turned to Dale.

"What do you do with the key when you're done, Dale?" he asked. Dale pursed his lips and didn't hide his amused grin.

"Just throw it in a mailbox, Doc. The address is printed on them. No postage required," Dale said.

"Oh. Dum de dum dum dum," Doc hummed, a perplexed look on his face as he drove away in his old green Plymouth.

I parked in the garage back of the jail. I was late for lunch, having responded to a call about a trout fisherman who had drowned in Duchee Creek. I stopped momentarily on my way to the jailhouse and played in the sandbox with Susan. Helen, checking on her whereabouts, came to the back steps.

"Oh, there you are. I didn't notice you drive in," she said.

"Susan and I are going to dig to China," I said.

"I hate to interrupt your fun," Helen replied, "but there's a nice old lady waiting for you in the office. She looks so sweet, almost like the picture of Grandma Moses. I asked her in for cake and coffee while she waited, but she said she didn't want to be a bother." I walked to the kitchen with Helen and poured myself a cup of coffee to take to the office. I noticed some left-over creamed chicken on the stove.

"Save me some of that," I said. "I'll be right back after I talk with Grandma Moses."

When I entered the office, the nice old lady was sitting silhouetted in the office window, with her back to my rolltop desk. Her knit shawl was draped around her shoulders, partially covering a tattered gray sweater. Cinnamon-brown finger curls protruded from the sides of a faded lavender scarf tied under her trembling chin. A white kerchief with a border of pink petunias was clasped in her wrinkled hands resting in the lap of her print housedress. She sniffled and dabbed at tears welling in her eyes as I set my coffee cup on the desk.

Helen was right. "Poor sweet Grandma Moses," I thought. Sunlight filtered by the giant walnut tree beyond the window made ideal lighting. A perfect picture for an art museum, I thought.

"I'm Sheriff Haugerud," I said, thinking what a shame that a nice lady like this would have troubles. "What's your name?"

"Stella," she softly sniffled.

"What's bothering you? Can I help?" I asked. I thought her poor heart must be broken over something. Stella dabbed at her eyes again, and blew her nose into the hankie. Then her facial features tightened and her eyes swam up above the edge of the ponding tears and gazed distantly for a moment before she spoke.

"It's that Goddamn, asshole son-in-law of mine, Dakota Wilson," she roared, in a loud voice I was sure could be heard in the kitchen. I jumped backward. "The little weasel son-of-a-bitch is always drinking with that shit-for-brains brother of his. He didn't come home for chores last night and I had to milk the Goddamn cows again. I want that little prick off my farm." She pounded her fist on my desk. "Now!" she shouted. A stapler fell off the desk and I retreated another step. Her eyes were hot, focused directly on me. "And he's been stealing my hay. He says he hasn't, but there was pigeon shit all over the top row and that's gone. He's a dumb little bastard, he is. You've got to do something with him, Sheriff."

She calmed down and gave me directions to her farm after I promised to come out soon and have a talk with Dakota. But I got busy and didn't get there soon enough, because the next day, at five o'clock in the afternoon, Stella called.

"Sheriff, come out here and get Dakota Wilson. He's drunk again and the little bastard threatened to shoot me," she said. I told her I'd be right out. I'd never met Dakota Wilson before, but when I pulled into the farm drive I was met by a lanky, even-featured man about five foot five. The brim of his cap was turned up and blood was dripping from a three-inch slash in his forehead. Unsteady on his feet, he stopped and leaned against a tree.

"The old bitch hit me with a neck yoke," he slurred, a dribble of snoose marking the corner of his mouth.

"Are you Dakota Wilson?" I asked.

"Sure am. What you gonna do about the old bitch what hit me?"

"You mean Stella? Where is she?"

"She's up in the house. Come on, let's go git her. Throw her sorry ass in jail for assault." Dakota plodded toward the house.

"Wait up a minute, Dakota," I said. There were a lot of things that needed to be understood before I went to the house with Dakota.

"When we get to the house, you speak only when I'm speaking to you and only to me. You understand, Dakota?"

"Goddamn right, Sheriff. You're the boss. We'll show that old heifer."

Stella was sitting at the end of the kitchen table just inside the door when we entered the house. Near the middle of the table sat a rather plump, younger-looking woman, wearing a washed-out, long-sleeved dress with a lace collar turned yellow with age. She was rocking a small baby in a homemade bassinet on the table. Dakota sheepishly took a seat at the far end of the table opposite Stella.

"I'm Sheriff Haugerud," I said to the woman rocking the baby.

"I'm Joleen, Dakota's wife," she said.

"Well," I said, addressing the group, "I think it might be best if I get a point of view of this situation from each one of you, but no arguing." I thought perhaps I could manage the predicament in a rational and studied fashion.

"Get the squirrelly little son-of-a-bitch out of here, Sheriff," Stella growled.

"Look at her, Sheriff," Dakota said. "What do you think that old battle-ax looks like? A Goddamn big capon is what she looks like. A big fat chicken with the nuts cut out, that's what she is." Of course, Stella didn't take kindly to this statement, and bedlam broke loose. I held my hand up for quiet.

"Hold on here, one at a time. Speak just to me. And remember, no arguing." My idea of a deliberate, rational approach to the case totally disintegrated when Stella, among other things, accused Dakota of having sex with the cows. And Dakota in turn accused Stella of doing it with the bull. Joleen and the baby sat quietly. I didn't dare leave the farm with both Stella and Dakota there, so I took Dakota in for being drunk and finished my investigation the next day while he was sobering up. Dakota had in fact sold the hay, but, since he'd helped put it up, there was a question whether it was outright theft or not. After Dakota got the booze out of his system, the family made up, and it was nearly six months before I got another call from Grandma Moses.

Early December, 10:30 A.M., Deputy Turner and I, on our way back to the office from a burglary investigation, received a call from Helen on the two-way radio.

"A rather distraught lady called and wants you to stop and see her," she said. The location was nearby, a farm in an area we called the "Holy Land"—a conservative district dominated by the influence of the Dutch Reform Church, where even youth softball was prohibited on Sunday.

When we arrived at the farm, a heavy, pear-shaped man, five-foot-three and wearing two pair of overalls, a heavy mackinaw, and a fur cap with earflaps tied under his chin, came from the barn to greet us. "Go in the house and talk to the wife," he said.

"What's the problem?"

"Just talk to her," he said, and walked back to the barn.

At the house a lady answered my knock, introduced herself as Martha, and ushered us into the kitchen. She was sixty-something, about five feet tall, gray-haired, heavy, and pear-shaped, like her husband. She kept a good house—frilly blue and white curtains on the windows and, oh my, the smells in that kitchen! Coffee had just reached its peak flavor on a wood-burning cookstove. A warmed stick of green cedar in the wood box added to the aroma. I detected the scent of fresh, home-baked bread. Blueberry muffins and homemade strawberry jam beckoned from the table. I began to salivate. Martha must have just popped the lid on that strawberry jam. And we'd been out since five that morning, without breakfast.

"You'll have some coffee, won't you?" she asked.

"Sure," I said, taking a seat at the table, getting comfortable. "Tell us your problem."

"It's the rays," she said. "That Dr. Nehring and Dale Thauwald come out here just at dusk and they shine rays at the house. Hot amber rays that come right through the walls. They generate heat, but they haven't started any fires." Martha poured our coffee; the cups and saucers were a blue and white pattern, like the curtains. Turner pushed his chair back from the table. I sipped my coffee, as flavorful as the aroma.

"Help yourself to a muffin," Martha said. "There are buns here on the counter. I just took them from the oven. There's only one place I'm safe when the rays come through the walls," she continued. "Here, let me show you." Reluctantly I left my muffin and coffee and followed Martha as she led us to a room just off the kitchen.

"This is our bedroom," she said, opening a white painted door. It was black as midnight in there. She turned on the light, a single, twenty-watt bulb in the ceiling, covered with a small brown grocery bag. The walls, windows, and ceiling were covered with layers of black roofing paper. Martha shut the door and turned off the light. You've never seen black like this. The construction-site-like smell drowned out all the fragrance from the breakfast table.

"I make Earl stay in here with me when the rays are on," she said from somewhere in the room. Turner opened the door and stepped out.

"Doc Nehring and Thauwald, eh?" I said. "How do you know it's them?" The strawberry jam and bread aromas drew me back to the table like a magnet. I sat down. Turner frowned and waved his hand as if to warn me away from the food. I put butter and a healthy portion of jam on my muffin and took a bite. Turner shook his head. He hadn't touched his coffee. Martha put the warm buns on the table. They were whole wheat.

"I heard that tune he always hums when I'm at his office, and the car looked like his green Plymouth, and there was laughter. Thauwald's laugh," Martha said.

"Does Earl feel the rays and see these people, too?" I broke open a bun, put on a pat of butter, watched it steam and melt, and licked my lips.

"No, Earl says he doesn't see or feel a thing."

I spread a generous portion of jam across the melted butter on the bun, took a bite, and sipped my coffee. "Ah ... this is a treat," I said.

"Oh ... there's other little things, but it's mostly the rays," Martha said. She poured more coffee in my cup. Turner declined.

"Mind if I smoke?" I asked.

"Oh, no, go right ahead. Earl smokes." I finished my coffee and cigarette while we talked. I was refreshed, content. Turner looked nervous. Before leaving, I told Martha I'd talk to Dr. Nehring and Mr. Thauwald. I didn't think she'd have a problem with them anymore.

Earl motioned to us from over by the barn as we came from the house.

"What do you think?" Earl pulled his earflaps up so he could hear better.

"Let me think about this," I said. "I'll be in my office tomorrow. Why don't the two of you stop in and see me about ten." Earl said that would be okay as long as Martha would come with him.

"How'd you dare eat that stuff?" Turner asked as we turned out of the driveway. "She's nuts. It might be poison."

"What's a little poison when it comes to good country cookin'?" I chided. "Look at old Earl: he's fat as a woodchuck."

I saw Dr. Nehring in the Victory Café later that afternoon on lunch break. I asked him to join me in a booth away from other people.

"What's this about you and Thauwald putting amber heat rays through this woman's house out in the Holy Land?" I said, and told him Martha's story.

"Oh, she's nuts," Doc said. "I've been their doctor for over fifteen years. Maybe they're a little mad at me now. The last time they were in, a couple of months ago—you know how fat they are and their shape—well, Earl said they couldn't find a position so they could have sex. You know what I told them, don't you?" I shook my head and looked down at the table, knowing something bizarre was coming.

"No, Doc, I don't know. What did you tell them?"

"I told Earl to put a lead pipe on it."

The next day, after a short conversation in my office, Martha looked at me.

"You're the sheriff. What are you going to do about this?" she asked.

"Have you ever thought of seeing a psychiatrist?"

"Psychiatrist! Do you think I'm crazy, Sheriff?"

"Maybe we're all a little crazy, Martha," I said.

"Crazy, huh?" she said. "Nobody has ever told me that before. Maybe you're right. I don't need to be locked up, do I?" I assured her that she didn't and gave her the name of a doctor in Rochester she might want to see.

I stopped at Martha's for coffee, bread, and jam a month or so later. Earl even came to the house. Martha said they'd seen the doctor once, but they had decided to try to get along the way things were. The black paper still lined the bedroom. Memories of the aromas in that kitchen drew me back several more times to check on Martha during my career. I was never disappointed.

D. T.'s and Alcoholics

Although I don't believe that there was necessarily a cause-and-effect connection, alcohol consumption was the predecessor of a good share of the dealings we had with people, whether it was burglary, theft, domestic abuse, or other law violations. Alcohol abuse caused endless problems, including delirium tremens on withdrawal. The onset of the D.T.'s was unpredictable, and the severity of the episodes varied widely. Some scared the drinker straight, some included humorous events, and others were fatal.

During one episode of note, Eli Enger, a fifty-five-year-old high school math teacher and former semipro baseball player, well educated and articulate, had been drinking steadily nearly all summer. The court, after an inebriety hearing, committed him to the state hospital at Willmar. I was to deliver him to the hospital, a five-hour drive each way. Helen accompanied us. She and I planned to stop for dinner at Michael's Restaurant in Rochester on the return trip. It was her favorite place for eating out and brought back fond memories. We had dined there on our second date.

Eli was pleasant company, an interesting conversationalist. He told us of his one opportunity pitching in the major leagues, as well as other stories about semipro baseball. He looked rather dapper, dressed in a navy blue sport coat, white shirt, tie, and tan trousers. Occasionally, he turned and talked to Helen in the back seat. They seemed to hit it off well. There were no outward behaviors to indicate anything amiss with the man's character.

Three hours into the trip, shortly after a rest stop, a cup of coffee, and a fill with gas, Eli reached out an arm's length toward the windshield and appeared to pluck something from the air between his thumb and two fingers. He looked at it momentarily, then tucked it in his shirt pocket.

"What's that, Eli?" I asked.

"White feathers," he said. "I thought they might bother your driving. I'll just put them in my pocket as I see them." I knew it was the D.T.'s.

He began searching in, around, and under the seat for something.

"I lost my ring and my wife's ring, too," he said, turning to Helen. "Maybe it's back there. I rode back there when Neil brought me in from home." Helen searched for the rings in the back seat. I didn't want to tell her Eli was hallucinating, because I knew I would get an argument to the contrary from Eli, and Helen wouldn't know what to believe. This was her first incident with anyone experiencing delirium tremens.

Eli discontinued his search for the rings, turned and looked slyly at me out of the corner of his eye, then reached into the inside pocket of his suit coat and acted as if he were bringing out a bottle. He unscrewed the cap, lifted his head, cupped his hands around the imaginary bottle, and took a long drink. "Ahhh," he said, and screwed the cap back on the bottle and placed it in his suit coat pocket.

"Better throw that bottle out, Eli," I said. "We're getting close to Willmar."

Eli rolled the window down; like a professional mime, he reached in his pocket, seized the bottle, threw it out, and rolled the window up again. I saw Helen in the rearview mirror, sitting on the edge of the seat, her blue eyes darting from Eli to me and her hand cupped over her open mouth.

Eli picked a few more feathers from the air and put them in his shirt pocket while he told us a story about one of his best math students.

"Watch out. Watch out, Neil!" he said suddenly, craning his head forward and pointing.

"What is it, Eli?" I asked.

"Elephants! Elephants crossing the road up there."

"They aren't pink, are they, Eli?"

"No. They're the regular color. Gray," Eli said.

At the hospital, Eli was polite and courteous to the staff when we went through the admittance process.

That evening over dinner, Helen had a good laugh at herself for helping Eli search for the rings. She said she never knew people could seem so normal while hallucinating. She found out for herself about hallucinating many years later, when she had an adverse reaction to cafergot, a medication prescribed for her migraine headaches. I had a difficult time convincing her that there weren't "cute little elves" gathering around to listen as she played the piano.

I observed all kinds of incidents with the D.T.'s—everything from bugs swarming out of the wastebaskets to feces being thrown around the cell. One incident occurred as I conducted a routine check of the jail. Our prisoner population was four, none charged with a serious crime. All sat at the table in the main area for the noon meal. I joined them for a chat. Harold, a slim, healthy-looking man of thirty-nine, had been in jail five days for drunkenness. When I brought him in, in wretched shape, he'd called me all the obscenities a drunk could think of. He was polite and respectful now, acting shy, quiet, and embarrassed about the circumstances of his arrest.

From past experience I was aware of Harold's drinking habits; once he started drinking, he didn't know how to quit. Once he called and asked us to corral him and take him before a justice and get him thirty days so he could dry out. We obliged. Despite a propensity for being terribly foul-mouthed when drinking and giving us some resistance when we brought him in, Harold was a friend, one of our regulars. His language and bravado caused him to get punched out in a tavern once in a while, but I don't recall him ever striking anyone.

I sat at the dining table and visited with Harold about the farm family he worked for. We were having a nice, normal conversation. Suddenly, Harold, without changing his voice or demeanor, began talking to the floor.

"What's going on, Harold?" I asked.

"The face. I'm talking to the face," he said matter-of-factly.

"What face, Harold?" I was always surprised by the sudden onset of D.T.'s.

"The one in the floor. Don't you see her?"

"No, I'm afraid I don't. Tell me about her. What does she look like?"

Harold looked at me, puzzled, and responded in an even voice, "You really can't see the face, can you?" He paused, staring at the floor. "It's there in that circle where the cement changes to onyx and polished agate. She's talking to me. See her lips move? She looks something like my mother, but it's not." Harold continued his conversation with the face for nearly five minutes. The face was gone as quickly as it came and our conversation returned to normal. When Harold finished his meal he cocked his head to one side and cupped his hand about his ear.

"Well, will you listen to that," he said.

"What?"

"The band. Don't you hear the band music?" Harold walked over to the window and looked out through the bars to the street. He saw, in the street outside, a high school marching band in red and white uniforms led by baton-twirling majorettes. They were marching back and forth in the street playing and marching to

Sousa's "El Capitan." Harold lingered at the window, keeping time to the music for nearly fifteen minutes. Then the band disappeared and was replaced by a truck backing up to the jail.

"Watch out!" Harold suddenly shouted.

"What now, Harold?" I asked.

"The people in the truck are hooking a chain to the jail. They're going to pull it away." When the imaginary chain on the imaginary truck jerked the building, Harold fell over backward, knocked himself out, and cut his head.

I called Doc Nehring. He stitched up Harold's head and gave him a vitamin B shot. There were no recurrences of the D.T.'s or complications from the fall for Harold, and he served another ten days. I don't recall that he ever returned to jail after that experience.

The most serious episode with the D.T.'s also began quite unexpectedly. Helen had just told the kids to turn off the TV and go to bed when one of the jail inmates began pounding on the inside of the dumbwaiter. She asked me to see the girls upstairs to their bedroom and she'd find out what the "other babies" wanted. Her patience was wearing thin with the immaturity of most prisoners. We'd popped corn earlier in the evening. Helen, gathering up the popcorn bowls from the living room, went to the kitchen and opened the dumbwaiter door. The dumbwaiter, in addition to conveying food to the prisoners, was also used as an after hours communication conduit from the jail. By now we'd learned that prisoners are generally nocturnal.

"What do you want?" she asked, obviously agitated by the intrusion. It was always something; someone wanted aspirin, or needed to call home, complain about the food, or talk to the sheriff.

"Neil better get up here right away," a man called down from the jail. "That guy Collin he brought in this afternoon is literally climbing the walls. He's going to get hurt."

It was Friday; the probate judge had issued an order to have Collin picked up and held in jail until Monday for an inebriety hearing. A concerned friend had filed the petition. Collin had worked at the bank in his hometown since he was twenty-two. He was well liked and respected, but he got to drinking too much— way too much. He never caused any trouble, he just drank. Last year, at age thirty-eight, he'd lost his job.

I rushed to the jail and let myself into Collin's cell area. Collin had climbed the bars of his cell to the ceiling. He began to lose his grip, so I positioned myself beneath him and broke his fall. His clothes were drenched with sweat. I asked two other prisoners to bring mattresses from unused bunks and watch over Collin while I went for bath towels from the storeroom. We spread the mattresses about the floor of the cell area in case Collin fell again. He sat on his bunk wringing his hands while I wiped the sweat from him. Then, before I could stop him, he grabbed a mattress and the soaked towels I'd used to wipe the sweat from his body and retreated to the corner of the cell.

"Get over here quick, Neil," Collin cried.

"What do you want, Collin?" I asked.

"Can't you see? The flood has undermined the schoolhouse. It's teetering on the brink of going into the river. Get over here with me and the kids." He pointed to the towels and mattresses: they were the children. "We need you for balance."

He described a desperate scene. I can still see it in my mind: a one-room schoolhouse with a raging river, at flood stage, tearing the earth from beneath it. It was teetering on the riverbank about to be swept away, and it was up to Collin to save the children.

"Knock a hole in the back wall and let the children out," he shouted. "I'll jump in the water and hold the school up till you get the kids out." Collin ran to the opposite corner of the cell compound, jumped as if jumping off a ledge, and began pushing upward on the top bunk of the cell. Standing in the raging river, straining with all his might, he held the schoolhouse up, sweat pouring from his body. Only after I told him that I had all the children out to safety did he stop straining against the steel bunk. He rested on the lower bunk momentarily, while I wiped him down with clean towels. Then he began climbing the walls again.

I stayed in the cell with him the rest of the night, breaking his falls and helping him through nightmarish hallucinations. The worst episode occurred at four in the morning, when two of the wet towels on the floor became little babies lying on a railroad track. The bars on the side of the cell were a locomotive building up steam, creeping toward the babies. Collin pushed on the bars, holding the locomotive back until the cords on his neck turned purple and swollen; rigid as concrete reinforcement rods. Sweat ran from his face like rain. The muscles of his arms were knotted as hard as oak limbs. I thought his teeth might break any moment from the clench of his jaw. He pushed against the train for more than twenty minutes before falling to the floor, drained of all energy and nearly his life.

A deputy relieved me at 8:00 A.M. It took me most of the day to prevail on the county attorney and the probate judge to have an emergency hearing so I could take Collin to the hospital at Willmar immediately. Doc Nehring finally convinced the judge it was an emergency; a hearing was held, and Collin went to the hospital.

Collin died seven days later at the Willmar State Hospital from cirrhosis of the liver and other complications of alcoholism. He was thirty-nine.

The County Fair

Annual county fairs are a long tradition in Fillmore County, beginning as far back as 1859. For decades, 4-H projects and exhibits have been the core and mainstay of the fair. My first 4-H exhibit, in 1939, was Barred Rock chickens; next it was a Poland China hog, and, finally, a Black Angus heifer. Once I even got to stay overnight upstairs in the 4-H building. Our thrill of the evening was spying on the girls as they were getting ready for bed, squinting through a small hole in the partition between the boy's and girl's dorms that one of the guys had made with his jackknife.

As late as the fifties and sixties, the grandstand shows were for many a once-a-year opportunity to gather with immediate family, uncles, aunts, cousins, and neighbors to observe trapeze artists, acrobats, jugglers, trained animal acts, and up-and-coming country singers, some of whom became nationally famous. But the draw, the spice, the atmosphere of the fair was the carnival. The carnival was what marching bands are to parades, what sage is to dressing, what tail feathers are to peacocks.

Tradition called for a walk through the midway, listening to professional barkers depicting the unbelievable but true freaks of nature that for a quarter's admission waited to astonish you just inside the tent.

"Hurry, hurry, hurry, step right up here!" the barker shouted. "Get your ticket to see the snake woman.

She walks, she talks, she crawls on her belly like a reptile. Inside this tent, right here, you'll see a three-headed calf, the world's fattest man, a bearded lady, and, for an additional fifty cents, if you are over eighteen, you can see a real live human hermaphrodite."

And across the way another barker on stage, in front of the Hootchy-Cootchy girly tent, shouted, "Come out here, Dolly, give the boys a little sample." Dolly, a buxom, long-legged blonde with a bit of wear on her, parted the tent flap and bounced onto the stage. "Ah," the barker continued, "that must be jelly because jam don't shake like that." Dolly gave a couple of bumps and grinds to a drumroll and the last thing seen as she reentered the tent was an extended posterior. "Come inside and watch her dance, boys. She dances on her right foot, she dances on her left foot, and in between she makes her living. Step right up, boys. The first ten tickets are half price," the barker said.

Along the midway there were age and weight guessers, a chance to show your strength by ringing the bell on the muscle machine and win a cee-gar, fortune-tellers, and tents with exotic reptiles from as far away as Australia and Africa.

For adults, the walk through the midway was true festival, a time for greeting friends and neighbors with a smile and visiting with others you might hardly say hello to on the streets in town.

For young children, it was pony rides, carousels, merry-go-rounds, and a face full of cotton candy.

For teenagers, thrill rides, flirting, guffawing, and giggling.

For the sheriff, though, it was something akin to a high-wire act—to police the fair and keep the carnies and the carnival in line with the diverse tastes of the community and balance law enforcement with the wishes of the fair board. In the fifties and sixties, sprinkled throughout the midway were a multitude of illegal gaming scams.

The owner of the show made it a priority to schmooze each member of the fair board, giving out free ride tickets for them to distribute to family and friends, in hope that things would go well for him when something went wrong. Something always went wrong in the carnival business, especially carnivals that pushed the limits of propriety as well as the limits of legality.

In 1959, the first year I was sheriff, I thought it best to learn everything about carnivals as fast as I could. The show's owner, K. J. Moran, a dressy type who drove a yellow Cadillac, came to my office the day before the fair with a proposal that, luckily, I didn't fall for. K.J. said effective law enforcement was essential to his success at the fair, and it would be difficult for him to put on his shows without our presence. He understood how being at the fair would take extra time from my busy schedule and offered me a hundred dollars cash for my being inconvenienced. No strings attached. Politely refusing his offer, I told him to go ahead and operate in his usual manner. During the first evening I made my rounds through the midway. At 11:30, I knocked on the door of K.J.'s trailer.

"I'd like to come in for a minute," I said. He ushered me in and invited me to sit down. I set a fifth of Seagram's Seven Crown whiskey in the middle of the table.

"Have a drink," I said. "No strings attached." He looked at me rather curiously and combed his hands through the mop of curly brown hair on his head before getting two glasses from the cupboard and my choice of mix from the refrigerator.

"My wife, Daphne," he said, motioning to a rather statuesque, colorfully dressed red-haired woman sitting in an upholstered chair by a reading lamp.

"Good evening, ma'am," I said.

"Nice to make your acquaintance, Sheriff," Daphne said, nodding. "Can I get you a snack with your drink?"

"No, thank you," I said. "I think K.J. and I will just have a little drink talk." K.J., his forehead a map of wrinkles, screwed another puzzled look on his face.

"Something's wrong with this picture," he said. "I'm supposed to be the guy with the booze and the proposition. You shaking me down, Sheriff?" Daphne opened the book she'd been holding, extricating herself from the conversation.

"No, I'm just looking for a quick education. Nearly every game on the midway is a scam. I need to know how they all work."

"They're all skill and luck, Sheriff."

"Bull," I said. K.J. sat silently, as if we were playing chess and it was my move.

"Games in tents number 3, 5, 7, and 8 don't open in the morning," I said. K.J. took a drink, lit a cigarette, and breathed the smoke out through his nose.

"Okay, where do we start, Sheriff?" he said.

"The game where the five balls roll down an incline and settle into an indentation with a number by it."

"Games like these are called controlled games. Here's how this one goes. The mark, that's what we call a player we suck in by a free chance, needs for the numbers where the ball settles to total thirty-six before he can score. The odds of this happening are nearly a million to one. The operator gives the mark a fast count [the operator counts the total and picks up the balls before the mark knows what's happening], making him believe he scored four points when he didn't score at all. The mark needs seven and one-half points to win in three rolls. He's led up to seven points with fast counts. Being a gracious soul, the operator says, 'Too bad, but I'll give you one more chance to reach seven and a half and double the prize money. For twenty bucks you can roll again and the prize is a hundred—all you need is a half point.' From now on the operator slowly totals the numbers so the mark can watch. For fifty bucks he increases the prize to two hundred bucks for the last half point. The mark never scores the last half point, but we have a shill who works for us come by and win big once or twice a day," K.J. explained.

It was well past midnight before K.J. had explained all the games to me.

"We don't have fortune-tellers," he said, "but, for future reference, if a carnival brings them in, remember, often a good portion of their action comes from picking pockets." We made an agreement that, for this year, the maximum take from any mark would be twenty dollars, only five if he had a wife or kids with him. If complaints came to my attention, all money would be refunded immediately, without question. K.J. kept his word, but never brought his carnival back to Fillmore County.

My education came in quite handy during the following year. On the afternoon of the second day of the fair, Dakota Wilson, one of my recurring jail customers, with half a snoot full, the bill of his cap turned up, and looking like a bewildered banty rooster, approached me on the grounds.

"A gypsy at the fortune-telling tent picked my pocket, took my billfold. It had eighty bucks in it," Dakota slurred.

"How do you know, Dakota?" I asked, and took him aside to hear his story. It seems during the lengthy telling of Dakota's fortune, the teller, a rather well-endowed lady, had the misfortune of having her upper garment, a buttonless wrap, come undone, nearly to the waist, exposing bare breasts.

"Before long," Dakota said, "they were right in my face. After my fortune I left the tent and went to play bingo. When I reached for my billfold it was gone. The gypsy must've took it."

"What was your fortune, Dakota?" I asked.

"Can't remember," he said sheepishly.

"Well, you better sober up and go home. I don't want to be called out to your place tonight like I have in the past. I'll check this out and contact you tomorrow."

I went to see Kirk, the carnival owner, a stubby, greasy-looking man with unruly hair who talked to me through the fly-laden screen door of his trailer.

"We have a problem," I said. "The fortune-teller's tent has to close and we need a man's billfold and eighty dollars back."

"What are you talking about, Sheriff!" he exclaimed. I filled him in on the details. He banged the door a few times to chase the flies away, then stepped outside, letting the door slam behind him.

"You don't have any proof. Are you prejudiced against gypsies, Sheriff?" he shouted. I knew the man was not going to cooperate.

"My only other alternative is to shut down every game on the midway."

"You can't do that, Sheriff. I'll go to the fair board. If you shut the games down, I'll shut the whole show down and pull out." I knew I wasn't getting anywhere, so I told him to shut down the fortune-teller's operation, and if I didn't have the billfold and money back by the next morning, everything was going down.

At four that afternoon, Moppy Anderson, our state representative and longtime treasurer of the fair board, summoned me to a meeting with the board and Kirk. They wanted to work something out. Kirk assured them that he had known the fortune-teller and her family for many years. There had never been an incident like this before. I tried to explain, but Kirk, the consummate professional con, had the board thoroughly convinced he'd pull out if I didn't back off.

"If you shut this midway down you'll never get elected in this county again," Moppy said. Several of the board members nodded agreement. I looked at Kirk.

"The fortune-teller's tent stays closed. I want the billfold and money back by noon tomorrow or joints 3, 5, 7, and 9 are shut down." I scanned the board members. They were in a quandary: shutting down the midway would ruin their fair. Kirk had skillfully made me the scapegoat.

"I stand on my decision," I said, and went back to my office, wondering if I was doing right.

By noon the next day I'd heard no more. I walked through the midway and closed games 3, 5, 7, and 9. Some of the operators protested, saying they were perfectly legal, but when I told them exactly how they operated, they pulled their flaps. I was summoned to another fair board meeting. Kirk said he was pulling everything out the next morning. I held my ground over the loud and rancorous objections of Moppy and some of the board members.

At 4:30 that afternoon, one of the carnival workers, taking a break for a beer and a sandwich down by the river, found a billfold with Dakota's identification, but empty of money, and brought it to my office. I contacted Kirk at his trailer.

"Now, if Dakota had his eighty bucks you'd be back in business," I said.

"You're kind of a son-of-a-bitch, aren't you, Sheriff?" Kirk said. Then he turned to his wife, a scruffy-haired blonde smoking a long unfiltered cigarette and drinking black coffee. "Give the man eighty dollars," he said. After receiving the money, I allowed him to resume operations, but the fortune-teller's tent stayed closed. There was no further trouble during the fair.

Thereafter, the fair board had some difficulty getting certain shows to come to Preston, but those that did were very cooperative, and we always came to an agreement as to which types of games would operate. All controlled games were phased out within three years. I did keep one perk for myself, though. If I saw a poor family with a child who would really appreciate a teddy bear, all I had to do was nod toward the family and a barker would cry, "Step right up here and throw the ball; knock over the stuffed kitty, it's easy. Three throws for a quarter. Here, young lady, I'll give you one free chance." He'd hand the ball to a little girl, she'd throw, the cat would fall over before the ball got there, and the little girl would walk away with a puzzled look on her face, holding a giant teddy bear.

John, "the grass eater," stood leaning against the windowsill, staring at the lawn outside, absorbing nutrients through his eyes from the grass. It was Monday morning; I'd come up to the jail to bring him to court for a mental hearing. John weighed over two hundred and fifty pounds and hadn't eaten anything the entire weekend while awaiting his hearing.

He'd given the deputies quite a struggle when they brought him in on Friday night. During the tussle, with his legs wrapped around the yard pole, John also fastened a firm grip on one of the deputies' private parts, inflicting severe pain. The deputy returned pain for pain by twisting John's prune-colored, alcoholic nose, at which John seemed quite surprised.

"Are you abuse-ing me?" John questioned, in a decidedly Norwegian accent. After releasing his grip on the deputy, John was handcuffed, but even this wasn't enough to quell his resistance. Before it was over, the deputies trussed John's feet with a rope and ran it behind the chains on the cuffs. They basically hog-tied him, laid him in the back seat, and brought him to jail.

"It's time to go to court for your hearing, John," I said. "You're not going to give me any trouble now, are you?"

"Give me a minute to finish eating first," he said.

"Eating?"

"Yes, I get my nourishment from the grass. I draw

the nutrients from it through my eyes when I focus and concentrate on it." I told John to go ahead and finish his meal. True to his word, he discontinued his glassy stare at the grass after a minute or so. John seemed quite cooperative at this time, so the deputy sat in the back seat with him on the way to court.

Later, the deputies who had originally apprehended John took him to the Rochester State Hospital.

"What happens when you look at a cornfield, John?" they asked on the way.

"That's pig food. I don't look at 'em," he replied. "And I can't even glance at a car battery without getting sick," he continued. John had been living in his car the year round lately, even in thirty below zero temperatures. There was a layer of blankets a foot high in his back seat.

While checking John in at the hospital, the deputies noticed that John wasn't being watched very closely. They advised the attendants that John might need closer surveillance.

"We know our job," one attendant answered curtly.

That day John vanished from the hospital, and two days later the deputies had a repeat performance with him and returned him to the hospital. After an initial tussle he calmed down, and even offered to clean the deputies' wristwatches with the rays from his eyes. They were clean as a whistle before they got to Rochester. Later, we thought we were quite remiss in not having John teach us his methods of drawing nutrients through his eyes. A session in front of the liquor store might have been appropriate for our instruction.

Canton

We were often called to quell disturbances in Canton, a rowdy town of fewer than three hundred inhabitants, located in open farming country two miles north of the Iowa border. I was born and raised on a farm two miles west, and my mother was born in Canton in 1899. Her father, Mike Armstrong, an Irish tyrant of sorts, believed in laying the horsewhip to his children when they misbehaved—horsewhippings administered severely enough to lacerate the skin. I'm not sure what it accomplished, but three of his four sons turned out to be alcoholics. My mother toned down the whippings when it came to her children. Hers was a ritual more than physical punishment when she retaliated for our misbehavior. After committing an offense we were required to make our way to the willow tree, cut a switch at least six feet long, and bring it back to her for our whipping. When we balked or tried to beg off, there was always a helpful brother or sister around offering assistance—"Let me go get it, Ma, I'll get a good one." When we secured our own switch we were allowed to keep four leaves on the tip for cushion. The siblings always brought back a thick seven-footer stripped clean of leaves with the thin end cut back a few inches, so as to smart a bit more. Then they'd offer advice: "Whack the little whelp good, Ma." None of us boys wore a shirt in the summertime, so the switch was laid across our bare backs. Oh, the dread of selecting that switch! And the walk back to the house became torturously slow, as we tried to delay the inevitable sting of the limber rod. Mother's anger had mostly subsided by the time the switch was selected and we stood for our punishment. We never received a switching any harder than you'd receive with cedars in a Turkish bath. But each time she made us believe that the next time we'd be whipped to an inch of our life.

Gramp, as we called Grandpa Mike, was the drayman in Canton when Mother was young. She told us how, as a little girl, she danced the Irish jig with her father in the barber shop while he played the rattle bones. Then she'd jig solo while he played, and the patrons threw pennies and nickels to the floor, which she picked up when the dance was over. Gramp always took the money from her as soon as they were out of sight of the barber shop.

One day, while she was riding with him on the dray, he whipped the team into a gallop and raced the train for a quarter of a mile to the crossing so he wouldn't have to wait to cross. He'd been drinking and Mother was sure they were going to be killed, but they bounded across the tracks, scarcely ahead of the train, though the cowcatcher clipped the endgate from the wagon and nearly tipped them over.

When Mother was eleven years old, she took a job as a live-in hired girl in town, earning two dollars a month, working for a family with four young children. She never returned home to live, but Gramp demanded and received her weekly wages until she was sixteen.

Gramp abandoned his wife and family and went to live I knew not where. When I was young he'd stay at our house a few days at a time, most often over the fifteenth of August, Canton's Day Off. He'd walk or take the bus to our farm and tell my mother he'd be back later that night after the celebration. Gramp was a great storyteller. He'd give us each a Sen-Sen (a spicy licorice the size of a pin head), then tell us kids tall tales of men, bears, and little animals who could talk. He had his own original storehouse of Disney-like characters long before we ever heard of Disney. Our grandmother had moved to California where she lived with her son Buck (Leo). Every two years, Uncle Buck and Uncle Poot (Orville) came from California to attend festivities at Canton's Day Off . They'd stop by at our place on the way—usually pretty drunk. Neither of my parents drank, nor was liquor allowed in the house, so the uncles made frequent trips to their car. When they became overly intoxicated, my mother ordered them off the farm. My father more or less ignored them.

Uncle Poot spent several months with us one winter recuperating from a butcher knife wound in his back. He said it was an Indian who'd done it. I recall a lot of blood when he struggled into the house, and he was unconscious by the time my folks got him upstairs to bed. It was nearly a month before he was ever out of bed. We didn't have electricity or indoor plumbing then, so there was a bedpan and another pot for us to empty in the outhouse. We boys slept three in a bed for a while.

Canton's Day Off began as a church festival sponsored by the Church of the Assumption, commemorating the day of the taking up of the body and the soul of the Virgin Mary into heaven after her death. On August 6, 1892, children of the Church of the Assumption were playing outside the church during recess from summer school. They reported seeing a faint image of the Virgin Mary holding a baby in the round window of the steeple and immediately told the priest, Father Daniel Jones.

Word of the vision spread. In a few short weeks, Canton found itself in the midst of a full-scale economic and social boom. So many people poured into the village that special trains were run. By August 22, more than six hundred people had visited the vision at the church. People came not only to see the vision but also to be cured of their crippling illnesses. Those who were cured left their crutches behind as testimonial to the validity of the vision.

To stop the pilgrimages and the almost carnival atmosphere,

Bishop Cotter of Winona had the window removed and even closed the church for a time in 1892. Thus ended the Miracle of Canton. In 1968, when the church building was replaced, a room full of crutches still remained in the basement of the old church.

By the mid-1930s, the August 15 celebration had become a day for more traditional activities in the area—drinking, dancing, fighting, and drinking, in that order.

There was a time when the church considered closing because of the drinking, rowdiness, and lawbreaking. It was still a rough-and-tumble town when I was sheriff. The first man I ever arrested was from Canton, a man named Pike Clark. A filling station near Canton was on fire and Pike drove in among the firefighters, drunker than a skunk on Saturday night. I arrived on the scene in an unmarked blue 1950 Chevrolet, in civilian clothes and with a badge in my pocket that looked like it came from a Cracker Jack box. Pike was big, blurry-eyed, and mean. He just sneered at me when I showed him my badge and told him to get in the car.

"You think I'm going in with a young punk son-of-a-bitch like you?" he said. I was more than a little scared.

"Pike," I said. "You're under arrest for interfering with fire-fighters."

"Piss off, kid," he replied, and began walking away.

"Pike, I'm going to take ahold of your arm and walk you to my car. If you pull away or resist you'll also be charged with resisting arrest. If I need help with you, I'll get it. Either way, you're going with me."

"Keep your Goddamn hands off me," Pike said, but I was pleasantly surprised when he turned, walked to my car, and got in the front seat. We drove about three miles before he changed his mind and pulled the key out of the ignition. I coasted onto the shoulder of the road and stopped. Pike got out and began walking back toward Canton. I walked along with him for a few yards.

"Okay, Pike, I'll be leaving now, but I'll be back," I said. "I'll bring the National Guard with me if I have to, and you are going to jail—probably for a good long time."

"All right, Goddamn it," he said, "but you've got to call Bert White in Mabel when we get to Preston." Bert was an old-style banker who liked to drink a little and associate with the good old boys. Sometimes Bert banked out of his pocket, making loans on Main Street if somebody he met was a little short of cash and needed fifty or a hundred.

Pike didn't give me any more trouble, and I called Bert after we arrived at the jail. He okayed the bail, but Pike was so drunk I locked him up overnight and released him the next day pending a hearing.

One summer day in 1996, to jar my memory as I began writing these tales down, I took the back roads to Canton. When I walked into the Pub, the only tavern in town, eight or nine men filled the bar stools, including Palmer Peter Wangen, or Peter Palmer Wangen, I wasn't sure which—they're identical twins who lived near the place where I grew up. Their given names are Palmer Peter and Peter Palmer because their folks couldn't tell them apart. They are seventy-some now. I ordered a whiskey seven, and taking a fifty-fifty chance, I said, "Give Palmer a drink." It turned out I was right.

"Never drink that hard stuff," Palmer said. "I'll take a beer, though. Three-two beer is all I drink. Bought a half pint of whiskey one time when I was a kid. Made me sick."

The bartender set up the drinks. In the mirror behind the bar I saw the reflection of a tough-looking, square-jawed, gray-haired man with a mustache staring at me with a frozen face. He was sitting near the middle of the bar. When I turned to look at him, he smiled.

"You don't know who I am, do you?" he said.

"You look familiar, but I can't say your name," I said.

"Clayton Clark."

"For Christ's sake, Clayton, I didn't recognize you."

"You remember when you locked me in your hotel a few times, don't you? You locked me and Connie Black up one night. Took us in together. It's a good thing you put us in separate cells. He was going to kill me when we got to jail. He would have, too."

"I'll never forget that night," I said. "That was one of the dumbest things I ever did as sheriff. I took you both in all alone, no handcuffs, nothing. Stupid. Especially when I found out later what kind of guy Connie Black was."

"My brother, Pike, used to give you more business than me," Clayton said. "My old man's the one that ruined Pike; he should never have bailed him out on that first check he ever bounced. Pike's the reason I put the glass blocks in the lower part of the window on the tavern. He'd always get mad at me when he was drunk, so he'd go outside and put his fist through the window. I got tired of fixing it up. So the last time I put in a few rows of glass blocks on the bottom. Pike got drunk and went out and broke his hand on them. He really did."

"Pike lived a tough life," I said, remembering the time when Connie Black broke a pint whiskey bottle across the side of Pike's head, raked the broken glass down his face and neck, then took him outside and kicked his head into the cement curb in the street. Nobody in town dared to go near Connie to stop him until the ambulance came and took Pike to the emergency room in Rochester, where he nearly died that night. I wasn't called until the next day. I had a deputy along to help when we took Connie in that time. When we approached him on the street he was drunk. His face had taken on a brooding, menacing expression. His jaw jutted forward defiantly, the muscles of his neck were swollen like those of a pit bull, and he held his fists up, daring us to come near. The deputy and I rushed him. I ducked under his swinging fists, and we wrestled him to the ground and cuffed him behind his back. Then he rolled on the ground and snorted like a mad bull. When we struggled him into the car there was snot stringing from his nose and white froth like foam blowing from his mouth.

I got careless when I took him from the car in Preston. Connie made a savage kick at my groin, but, since he was handcuffed behind his back, his effort caused him to fall over backward and hit his head on the car frame in the open doorway.

The court ordered Connie to have a psychiatric examination, which took a month at a Rochester hospital. The report came back recommending that Connie not be incarcerated because it might disturb his personality.

Clayton waited patiently for a response, since my mind had drifted off; he had a mischievous look in his eye. I could tell he wanted some tales for the boys at the bar to hear, so I continued.

"You had the tavern across the street for a long time, didn't you, Clayton? I tell people about that place. Most taverns would cut you off or throw you out if you stood at the bar and drank beer till you pissed your pants. They say you pulled a garbage can up and put Lennie Whalan in it after he pissed his pants standing at the bar—then kept selling him more beer."

"I wouldn't do that; hell, Neil, you got it all wrong.... It wasn't Lennie Whalan, it was Billy Gossman." Clayton roared with laughter. The whole bar was listening and laughing with us. I finished my whiskey seven, glanced at the wide-eyed patrons at the bar, and ambled toward the door.

"Good to see you again," Clayton said. "Where you headed?"

"Maybe I'll take the back roads home ... stop off at Lilly's Amherst store for cheese and crackers and the latest gossip," I said.

Irvin Johnson, raking leaves and picking up walnuts in the back yard, leaned the rake against the side of the garage as Helen and I walked down the back steps and approached our car. He walked over and opened the car door for Helen.

"I hope everything goes good for you, Helen," he said. "I'll be serving another two weeks so I'll get to see the baby. I don't think I'll be back here again, though. I've learned my lesson for good this time."

Our son was born at 9:15 that night, October 13, 1962, at Saint Mary's Hospital in Rochester. The Mayo Clinic served as our family doctor now. Doctor Wagner, after becoming arthritic, had moved to a warmer, dryer climate in Arizona. Saint Mary's, one of the largest hospitals in the United States, was a stark contrast to the Harmony hospital, a converted seven-room house in Harmony's residential area, where Renee and Susan were born.

Helen never wasted much time delivering babies. When Susan was born, she was in no hurry to leave home. I had to practically drag her out of the house.

"Too early to go yet," she had said as I opened the car door for her. "It might be a false alarm." When we reached the hospital in Harmony, she told me she felt fine, so I let her off at the street. She was walking in through the front door of the hospital as I drove away to take Renee to my parents' farm; I was back in ten minutes and ushered directly into the delivery room by a nurse. The phone rang as I stepped into the room. Helen was on the delivery table. Doc Wagner's long arms on his six-foot-four frame reached the phone on the counter without disrupting his attendance to Helen.

"Be right there," I heard Doc say. He hung up the phone, turned back to the delivery table, and, like a magician, held a wet, wriggling baby up by the feet and gave it a slap on the behind.

"It's a little Susie. Everything is fine," he said, handing the baby to the nurse. "Come along with me, Neil, there's nothing you can do here." Doc tugged at my arm, leading me out the door. The next thing I knew we were traveling south out of town at 110 miles per hour in Doc's Ford Thunderbird.

"That phone call was Phyllis Orwoll down by Granger," Doc said. "She thinks her husband Emil had a heart attack. I've been treating him for heart trouble. She said he passed out."

Phyllis was partially correct in her diagnosis, and Emil had recovered consciousness by the time we arrived. Doc gave him a thorough checkup, administered some medication, decided he would be okay until morning, and told him to come in the next day for some further tests. I thought I was in as much danger as Emil just riding with Doc, who drove almost as fast on the return trip, but I survived, and Doc and I were back at the Harmony hospital less than an hour after we'd left. Helen was resting in her room, flushed and a little groggy from the mild anesthetic she'd received. Susie was doing fine.

Things were quite different at Rochester Saint Mary's. My request to be in the delivery room with Helen was denied.

"Oh my," the nurse said. "We don't allow that here." I paced in the waiting room, but not for long. The nurse was back in less than thirty minutes with the announcement that we had a fine baby boy. It was nearly an hour before they allowed me to see

Helen and the baby. Helen stayed another day. I picked up her and "Baby Boy Haugerud" the following morning at ten. We couldn't agree on a name, so our son was listed on the hospital records as "Baby Boy Haugerud." We'd worn a hole in the name card we were supposed to turn in, writing down and erasing name after name.

I'd parked the patrol car in the circle drive back of the hospital. By now we never gave a second thought to our family car with "Fillmore County Sheriff" stenciled on the front door and a red light on the roof, but when a nurse and I wheeled Helen and the baby down to the car in a wheelchair and I held the baby while Helen seated herself in the car, some onlookers near the entrance had puzzled looks on their faces. We left the city and drove south. The sun was shining in a cloudless sky, making for a glorious Indian summer day. The rugged, wooded hillsides were at their very peak of fall color: the sumac a bright burgundy, the poplar trees gold, the oaks a rust red, the elms a dark yellow, and here and there a sprinkling of green spruce and cedar. We stopped at Chatfield so Helen's parents, Sig and Avis, could see the baby. This was the first boy in their family. They were as proud as if they were the parents themselves. Children could never have grandparents finer than Sig and Avis. They gave us a gift for the baby, then bade us good-bye, and we continued our journey home.

The river ran clear, sparkling in the sunlight as we crossed the Root River bridge. Helen and I reflected on bringing a newborn baby home to a jailhouse. How far from reality it would have been to us when we first married. Helen held the baby close and said she couldn't help but think about Heidi when she went into the delivery room. We talked a lot about the past four years, how fast they had gone, and wondered if we'd still be in our jailhouse home after the upcoming election in November. I was somewhat concerned, but Helen never seemed to fret about things like that. When we were first married we had five hundred dollars between us, four hundred of hers and a hundred of mine. I worked as a carpenter for a dollar and a half an hour and no worry about our future ever entered Helen's mind.

"Things have gone pretty well for us," I said. Helen's eyes moistened and she nodded.

"I just love babies," she beamed.

It was different for me. They rather scared me when they were little. I couldn't wait until they could kind of sit up on their own. Renee had almost put us out of our minds when she was little. She had colic from the time we brought her home until she was almost three months old. She could vomit ten feet across a room, scream until we gave her more milk, and throw it up five minutes later. On several occasions she cried continuously and so convulsively that we called Dr. Nehring, who came to the house and had to medicate her to get her to sleep.

Susan, on the other hand, was a perfect baby. She slept the whole night through on her third night home and almost every night thereafter.

"How come we don't have a name for this boy?" I asked as we neared the city limits of Preston.

"I don't know," Helen said. "It seems like we've been so busy with all the prisoners, the election, and the two girls, and this guy came along before we had time to think."

"Sloan," I said. "How about Sloan?"

"Sloan? I've never heard of a Sloan. What kind of name is that?"

"It's a tough guy's name I read about in a western book."

"I don't like it." Helen didn't always catch on right away when I began to tease. They'd never teased in her home.

"Iron Eyes," I said. "Iron Eyes Haugerud, that's got a good ring to it."

"If I left it up to you . . . you really would, wouldn't you? You'd name him something like that." She hugged the baby to her. "Thomas," she said. "How do you like Thomas? Thomas Neil."

Renee, Susan, my mother, and the neighbor girl Mary were waiting for us when we arrived at the jailhouse. Mary, Renee's age, had
become like part of the family, sleeping over, popping in and out
at will, sitting on my lap for breakfast when she was four and five.
We loved her as if she were one of our own. Everyone helped get
Thomas Neil settled in his crib in the living room, and life came
around to a new normal in a few days.

The day began wonderfully. There had been no calls during the night, and Tom, four weeks old now, had slept the whole night through for the first time. I'd been downtown earlier and won my breakfast shaking dice at the community table in the Victory Café. It was unseasonably warm for early November, although there was a foot of snow on the ground. As I walked back toward the office I reflected a bit on Tuesday's election. I'd been reelected quite handily and was glad it was over. It was Thursday, and by ten o'clock, with most of my paperwork finished, I began thinking of the little respite I might have that evening, turning a card with the boys at the weekly stag night at the Harmony Golf Club.

At eleven, while on the phone confirming a sentencing hearing for Maynard Brown on a burglary charge, there came a knock on the jail door. The deputy scooted his chair back, hastened to the hall, and ascended the steps to the landing by the jail door. I tuned him out.

When I hung up the phone he was standing by my desk with a puzzled look on his face.

"That was Irvin Johnson. He says he's ready to finish some work in the yard he started the last time he was in."

I couldn't recall any unfinished project. Mildly suspicious, I told the deputy to bring him down to the office.

"I need to talk to you, Neil," Irvin said, a worried look on his face. Irvin looked past me out the window and rubbed the back of his neck with his hand. I walked him to the private office and closed the door.

"Maynard might be going to kill you, Neil," he said. He was looking straight at me now. "He's got a gun on him, up in the jail."

This grabbed my attention. "What the hell—where did he get that?" I asked. Irvin broke into a nervous, postdrinking sweat, unusual for the amount of time he had been in jail, I thought.

"It was a little over a week ago," he continued. "Remember when you brought that old guy, Larson, in for overnight? Well, we were all sitting around and he got to telling how he'd been jailed here back in the thirties. This Larson said he made an impression of one of the keys in a bar of soap when the sheriff laid the keys down to take a leak. Later, he was let out to chop wood and when he was in the shop he split open an old piece of water pipe and with a file made a key from the pattern in the soap. He never let anyone know about it and hid the key up in the angle irons near the ceiling. He wondered if it was still there, so he stood on a chair and slid a table fork along a slot in the angle iron and the key dropped out. He gave it to Maynard. It worked for the cell doors on the south side and the one used for storage."

"Oh, God," I said. Inside the storage room were old files, partly full whiskey bottles we'd taken off drunks, and, more important, a .38 caliber revolver a man had committed suicide with. There were five live rounds in the box with it.

"For cripes sake, Irvin," I said and began pacing the office. "Go on. There's more."

"I drank the whiskey," Irvin stammered. "I didn't dare tell till now." That explained why he appeared to have a nervous sweat.

"Does Maynard suspect you of anything?" I asked. I could hear the kids laughing and playing in the living room on the other side of the office wall.

"I'm not sure," Irvin said. "But I don't think so." I paced some more, and in the quiet I heard Helen rattling pans in the kitchen, preparing dinner.

"Maynard told me if he got sent up today he was going to kill you," Irvin said. That was a relief. If he was planning to wait until after the hearing, it gave us time. I figured sometime before two o'clock Maynard would want to clean up to look good for the judge. We devised a plan. When Maynard went to the bathroom, Irvin was to knock on the jail door and tell me he was ready to go back to work.

I locked Irvin up and informed the deputy of the situation. We'd have to wait. By now the savory aroma of Helen's vegetable soup had permeated the office. I'd never had old-fashioned hard dumplings in soup until after we were married. Early on she'd even fed me dumplings and milk once for a complete evening meal and I'd begun to wonder what the hell I'd gotten myself into. Now I'd come to love those dumplings. I detected the smell of onions, cabbage, rutabagas, and a meaty soup bone. I knew there would be carrots, potatoes, and celery, too. I'd suggested once she try some kohlrabi in the soup, but Helen just said, "Oh, ish."

I stepped into the kitchen and was drawn to the stove, where the soup was bubbling in a large kettle. I liked to drop the dumpling mix from the spoon into the boiling soup. I didn't tell Helen what was going on in the jail. We fed the prisoners, and I was on my second helping of soup when I heard the knock on the jail door. I jumped up and dashed through the office.

When we unlocked the jail door, the deputy and I rushed past Irvin to the bathroom. Maynard was shaving. We pinned him against the wall and I got the loaded .38 revolver from his waistband before he had a chance to make a move. He offered no further struggle. I told Maynard I wouldn't report the incident to the judge before sentencing. Maynard was young and scared, and I didn't want to jeopardize his chance for probation.

At two o'clock I took Maynard to the courthouse, where he received a sentence of three to seven years in the state reformatory. I had no sooner sat at my desk after returning Maynard to his cell when a clamor came from the jail.

"Sheriff, get up here, Maynard's cut himself," another prisoner yelled. I smelled blood as I let myself into the compound. During the last couple of years I'd gotten to know the blood smell quite well. Maynard had slit both of his wrists: one superficially, and the other was spurting blood from a nicked artery. The deputy went to call Doc Nehring while I clamped my thumb on Maynard's wrist to stop the bleeding. A razor blade lay on the floor.

Doc stitched up Maynard's wrists without benefit of anesthesia. Maynard was docile and uncommunicative during the process. On the way out, Doc stopped by to pay his respects to the other prisoners.

"You don't look like bad guys," he said. "I suppose you're just a bunch of drunks. Drunks are okay. I don't mind drunks. It's guys that write bad checks that I don't like. They should be strung up. Dum-ta-dum-dum-dum," he hummed. Needless to say, two of the men were in for writing bum checks.

Later a charcoaled steak, a couple of drinks, some loud talking, and a game of chance at the Harmony Golf Club provided the respite of the evening I had been longing for.

"Shut up and deal," cried the losers.

Tom turned out to be a good baby, except for having difficulty getting to sleep at night. If I laid him in his crib and patted his stomach he'd go to sleep, but I had trouble getting out of the room. There was a loose floorboard in the doorway that squeaked anytime I stepped near it. No matter how I tried to sneak out of the room, Tom would hear that board creak, wake up, and cry till I patted his stomach again. Telephones ringing, jail doors clanging—that didn't bother him, just that damn board creaking. I tried crawling on all fours to avoid the thing. That didn't work either. It took nearly a month of innovative experimentation before I learned to lay on my back and slide across the offending timber. Sometimes while making sure he was asleep I just lay on the floor reflecting.

Many things had happened and a lot of change had taken place during the last four years. I'd been re-elected. John Kennedy was president, and I'd learned that Helen liked to have the radio on playing music twenty-four hours a day. We made a compromise, and the radio would be turned off when I came to bed. It was hard to figure, though. Many times when I went out on a call at night Helen wouldn't even wake up. When I came back she'd still be sound asleep but the radio would be on. I think I heard "Blowin' in the Wind" by Peter, Paul, and Mary a thousand times. In 1961 the coal-fired furnace in the basement was converted to gas, relieving me of the nightly chore of shoveling coal into the stoker. This pleased Helen, too. It seems at times I'd forget about changing my footwear or putting on rubbers when shoveling coal and occasionally I'd carelessly track coal through the house. She hadn't cared for the coal dust that settled all about the house after a coal delivery, either.

Rose Connolly, a delightful, opinionated Irish lady, came by one afternoon a week to help Helen with housework and meal preparation for the prisoners; seventeen had been our highest count.

I had a second deputy now, and Helen, all 103 pounds of her, also performed the duties of a full-fledged deputy sheriff when needed—without pay, of course. In emergencies we enlisted her assistance as matron to frisk female prisoners and otherwise serve when transporting females.

One such emergency was the day Mrs. Culbertson, a rather sizable woman near seventy, went over the edge. She'd been acting rather strange; for example, she had been breaking into the German Lutheran church and playing the pipe organ for hours on end. The palms of her hands were just healing from burns she'd received placing them on hot stove lids. Not knowing what she'd done now to draw attention, we received a court order instructing us to take her to the Rochester State Hospital forthwith. She was wearing a floppy-brimmed straw hat and a flowing print grandma dress that extended to the top of her brown oxfords, and she was carrying a brown paper sack containing a half gallon of buttermilk when Deputy Turner and I apprehended her. We'd spotted her walking down the middle of West Main Street talking to God.

Though uncooperative and argumentative at first, once in our car she offered little resistance. Even so, a matron was required, so we pressed Helen into service.

Unable to find a baby-sitter, Helen brought the children along. Renee rode in the back seat with Deputy Turner and Mrs.

Culbertson. Susan and Tom sat up front with Helen and me. En route to Rochester, Mrs. Culbertson didn't have anything to say to us adults, but conversed freely with Renee and Susan, pausing during the conversation to sip her buttermilk from the carton—rather carelessly, I might add, as buttermilk dribbled from her mouth to her chin, where she brushed it away with the back of her hand and wiped it on her dress.

When we arrived at the hospital administration building, Turner stepped from the car and reached down to give Mrs. Culbertson a hand. Apparently she'd spilled a bit of the buttermilk inside the paper sack. The wet bottom gave way, the buttermilk container upended in her lap, and a pool of milk formed in her dress between her knees. To keep the milk from spilling, she grabbed the hem of her dress, swung her legs out of the car, and began vigorously shaking her garment, showering Deputy Turner from his waist to the top of his head with buttermilk, his face and hair receiving the lion's share of the fluid—all to the delight of Renee and Susan. A close observer might have caught a smile on Helen's and my faces also. After some choice words Deputy Turner managed a reluctant grin.

A few months later, Helen and I had occasion to take another mental patient, Sally, to the state hospital. Sally, like Helen, was in her early thirties and slight of build. As we left Preston she began talking nonstop in a monotone, interrupting herself to read every road sign. "Silos—Van Dale—For sale—Olmsted County 7 —Mile 41—Midland Co-op—Junction Olmsted County 129— U.S. Highway 52—Mile 42—No passing zone—Are you circumcised, Neil? Christ was circumcised. For Jewish people it is their religion—Junction 19—Olmsted County 43—Predmore—School bus stop ahead—Marion Road—Speed 50 miles per hour—Standard Oil—North 52—Speed 60—Rochester 6 miles—Reduced speed ahead—No passing zone—Speed 40—one cow by a cornfield—Do you know that Al Quie is our congressman and Harold LeVander is the governor?—two black birds—Speed 60— 55 at night—School bus stop ahead—Tasty Bread—No passing— Curtis Hotel—Do you believe in Christian Science? Mary Baker Eddy founded the Christian Scientists at the First Church of Christ Scientist, Boston, Massachusetts—Keep your powder dry —Be prepared—Don't shoot till you see the whites of their eyes— The hand is quicker than the eye—No left turn—U.S. 52 North— one dead dog on the road—State Hospital."

When we arrived at the hospital, Helen stayed in the car with Sally while I took the paperwork to the administration building. Then we drove to admittance building B. I'd experienced this pro-cedure many times. After passing through a pair of double doors at building B, we were met at the beginning of a long hallway by two burly male attendants in typical institutional white uniforms.

Momentarily overcome by "the divel mischief" (a small Irish devil) when the white coats approached, I handed the paperwork to the men and nodded toward Helen. The attendants, acknowl-edging my cue, tugged on Helen's sleeve.

Helen laughed, a rather nervous snicker, I thought.

I stepped away from her, frowned, and said, "Go along now. Don't give any trouble."

Helen jerked her arm away from the attendants, causing them to respond with a firm hold on both her arms. She dug in her heels, sliding along stiff-legged, before they lifted her off the floor. She craned her neck back at me, a grimace on her face. She shouted, "Neil! Neil! Neil!!!"

The attendants, familiar with such protests, continued on their way. Sally, understanding the irony of the situation, put her hand on my arm and looked on smugly. At the last moment, when the white coats were at the end of the hall, about to turn the corner with frazzled Helen, I shouted, "Wait a minute guys!" I shook my head and pointed to Sally. "This one!" I said.

I've previously mentioned that Helen wasn't used to being teased before we were married, and most often didn't appreciate teasing now. She was near tears—really steaming—and the attendants were well aware of it.

"You'll be lucky if you live through the night," one of them said to me, with a shake of his head and a sympathetic smirk, before returning down the hallway with a subdued Sally.

Poor Helen . . .

Poor Neil!

Friday morning before school, Renee heard the screen door on the porch slam as she came down the stairs for breakfast. Her second-grade classmate Mary Gross dashed through the back door with her book bag slung over her shoulder.

"Renee, Renee!" she said. "Irvin is sitting in a big hole in the jail wall out back. When I came by he said, 'Don't blame me, I didn't do it.'"

"He is not," Renee exclaimed.

"Yes, honest, he is," Mary said.

Helen set breakfast on the table. "There was a jail-break last night, Renee," she said. "Your dad is still out." The girls ran out to get the details from Irvin, who was sitting in the hole with his legs dangling to the outside.

On the previous day Helen and one of the prisoners, a young man in his late teens, had a tête-à-tête about the quality of his meals, and during the day exchanged notes on the dumbwaiter. For the evening meal everyone had roast beef, mashed potatoes and gravy, green beans, bread, and coffee. There was one exception. Helen placed jars of Gerber baby food—strained carrots, peas, and a jar of processed liver—on the dumbwaiter, along with a note that said, "This is for the baby." At seven, as I was ready to leave for men's night at the golf club in Harmony, a knock came from inside the dumbwaiter. There was a note with the empty baby food jars, which we chuckled over. "Better than your cooking anyway," it said. I should have opted to stay home and comfort Helen—she'd had a rather exhausting day—but of course I didn't. I cherished my Thursday evenings out, particularly the poker games that lasted until about two in the morning.

At eleven o'clock I was playing seven-card stud with the boys—had kings wired in the hole, and one showing, and another hole card to draw. Nearly everyone in the game had a nickname. Stoner, to my left, bet two stones. Cleaver, the butcher and resident king of blasphemy, slapped his cards down. "Son-of-a-bitch, I fold," he said, then muttered something about a pair of damn crucified frigging queens. Foggy, an old one-eyed trapper who'd served a stint at Graystone College at Saint Cloud during prohibition for running booze, paused and looked across the top of his cards. Jimnson Weed folded and took a sip of beer. I called the bet and was thinking of raising. Foggy focused that one steely gray eye on me.

"Don't let greed spoil your vision, boy," he rumbled with a voice deep in his chest.

Before I could respond, the club manager shouted from the bar.

"Neil, telephone. Urgent." I laid my cards on the table and went to the phone.

"Hello," I said. It was Helen.

"Ha ha," she said. There was glee in her voice. "You can put your cards down and come home now."

"Why would I do that?"

"Ha ha," she repeated cheerfully. "Four guys just broke out of jail."

"Finish my hand for me," I said to the manager. "Call all bets and hold my money till next week. I've got to go." Then I asked Helen to get on the two-way radio. "I'll be in the car in a second," I said and hung up the phone.

Now it seemed to me that for most young women, if they were

home alone with small children living in a jailhouse, their first reaction to a jailbreak might be fright. But somehow, the jailbreak provided Helen with a bit of sardonic humor. Maybe it was her way of getting even. Two weeks earlier I'd nearly had her committed at the state hospital as a joke. And tonight things had been pretty unsettled when I left.

Helen was on the two-way when I got into the car. She said Irvin Johnson and "the baby" didn't go with the others. Irvin had rapped on the dumbwaiter and told her about the breakout. He was afraid to tell until everyone had gone through the hole. I had her phone Lee Tienter, Preston's policeman, and Jim Knight, a schoolteacher who served as special deputy.

The first thing I noticed when I pulled into the driveway at home was a big hole in the brick wall of the jail. By the time I arrived, Lee and the deputy on duty were cruising the town. Jim Knight waited for me in the office. Jim wasn't yet thirty, his hair had begun to thin, and despite all his athletic activity as high school football coach and his intramural activity in basketball and softball, his midsection was beginning to show the effects of a hearty appetite and love of a few beers on occasion. He did retain the quickness and dexterity of his college quarterback days when need be—he could spear the last piece of cake from the dinner plate if anyone else made a covetous glance at it.

I alerted the surrounding law enforcement jurisdictions with a description of the escapees. Lee called in on the radio and said a black 1949 Chevrolet four-door was missing from the Preston Golf Club and presumed stolen.

Instinct is hard to define, but there are times when something enters my mind as if it were placed there in a form of communication I can't fully comprehend. This was one of those times. I knew exactly what I wanted to do and exactly where I wanted to go. I handed Jim a .30 caliber rifle from the gun cabinet and strapped on a .38 myself, something I very seldom did.

"Come on, Jim," I said. "Ride with me."

"Okay, where we going?" Jim asked.

"I have an idea. I'll tell you on the way."

The idea in my mind was a picture of a particular road in an area near the town of Fillmore, a country store with gas pumps out front, located near rugged wooded country with one-lane roads and bridges.

I didn't share the exact details with Jim. As we drove I told him we were not even to think about shooting at or near anyone. The guns were for show. We'd had long talks about guns and were in agreement about their use. We operated under a strict rule: no shooting unless you were absolutely sure your life was in imminent danger. And don't ever get yourself in the situation if you can help it. A few years earlier, while making an arrest, I had wrestled with a man named Larkin who had cut someone up with a broken beer bottle. I can't remember why I was wearing a gun then, but he went for my gun and got the safety strap loose on my holster. I knew if he got the gun he'd shoot me. I could get my gun out but I knew I wasn't going to shoot him. "What the hell do I have this damn gun on for?" I thought. I held Larkin off until I was aided by a friend who came out of the tavern. Between the two of us we put the handcuffs on him and took him to jail. I hardly ever wore a gun after that.

Jim and I turned off Highway 16, went through Wykoff, and drove south on a gravel road. One of the escapees had lived in this area few years ago. I turned west off the main road. We crossed the Root River and turned north onto a narrow dirt road about fifty yards from the river and crossed a one-lane bridge over a dry run. The road narrowed even more, and we squeezed by a huge elm tree growing on the road's edge. While rounding a slight curve, we met the '49 black Chevy nearly head on. It swerved to our left into a slight incline of a ditch, passed us, and went back up on the road again. It was a quarter of a mile before there was a place wide enough for us to turn around, so I slammed on the brakes, snapped the transmission into reverse, and gave chase. How ridiculous this must have looked, a 1960 Pontiac, backing up, chasing a 1949 Chevy. But the driver of the Chevy, in his haste, hit the huge elm tree. All four occupants bailed out and ran. Jim and I gave pursuit on foot.

"Crank off a couple of rounds, Jim," I hollered. He let fly with two rounds in the air from the .30–.30. The shots echoed through the valley. One of the escapees skidded to a stop; another took a swan dive over the riverbank. Jim took custody of the first offender and I ran to the riverbank. Escapee number two was in water and mud up to his waist, clinging to the side of the bank. About ten minutes later Jim and I marched the two culprits back to my car, where a third escapee sat on the hood of my car waiting, smoking a cigarette.

"Whoops, done it again," I thought. I'd left the keys in the ignition.

"Hi, Keith," I said.

Keith gave me a knowing smile and took a long drag on his cigarette.

The fourth escapee called from his parents' home and turned himself in a day later. We picked him up at their house.

Not the best way to end an election campaign.

Jack Hammervold at Hammervold Field admiring the flying club's Aeronca before its fateful flight.

Front view of the Fillmore County jailhouse. The sheriff's office entrance is on the right; the residence entrance is on the left.

VOTE FOR

NEIL S. HAUGERUD

Candidate For

SHERIFF

OF FILLMORE COUNTY

Married Veteran, with two children. Am 28 years old and have been a resident of Fillmore County all my life.

Experienced and Qualified for the Office of Sheriff

Prepared and Circulated by Neil S. Haugerud, Harmony, Minnesota

Neil's campaign card from the 1958 election, the only handout of the campaign.

Neil and Helen Haugerud in 1967, their last year at the jailhouse.

Susan and Renee waiting patiently behind the jail for Dad to take them on a Saturday trip to Lilly's store at Amherst. As so often happened, Dad got a phone call just as they were about to leave.

Tom, twenty months old, in the jailhouse kitchen helping Mom with dishes. Note the dumbwaiter door, partially open, in the upper left of the picture; the dumbwaiter was used for food service to the prisoners.

Neil and Karen Haugerud in 1966 in the kitchen of the sheriff's residence adjacent to the jailhouse.

Four Youths Flee Preston Jail; Two in Custody, Others Hunted

PRESTON — Two out of four youths who broke out of the Fillmore County jail here about midnight Wednesday were back under lock and key by 9:30 a.m. today and law officers from two counties were hot on the trail of a third at press time.

The quartet, three burglary suspects and one probation violator, escaped by using a pipe from a stairway railing to batter their way through the rear brick wall of their cellblock.

Captured by Sheriff Neil Haugerud about 5 a.m. today was ███████ 20, California, a burglary suspect. ████████ 19, Chatfield, also a burglary suspect, gave himself up about 9:30 a.m.

TWO STILL MISSING

Still missing are: ████ 18, Rochester, probation violator; and ████████ 18, rural Chatfield, burglarly suspect. Neither is armed.

████████ and ████████ were arrested just last Sunday in connection with a weekend burglary at Wykoff. ████████ had previously been convicted of burglary and was in jail for violating his probation.

The break-out was discovered about 12:30 a.m. when two other inmates of the jail began banging on their cells and making a great disturbance to attract the sheriff's attention.

When Haugerud came to investigate all the rumpus, the inmates said the four youths had just escaped minutes ago. The boys covered the railing pipe with a blanket to reduce noise of their battering on the wall.

The brick wall is 18 inches thick but its mortar is "soft as sand" in the center. A hole just big enough to squeeze through was made by the escapees.

Sheriff Neil Haugerud Directs Search

Neil on the two-way radio, checking in with Helen, who was left in charge of the office, house, and jail while the search was on.

Doc Nehring posing with a catch of walleyes at his favorite resort on Mille Lacs Lake. Photo courtesy of Dr. John Nehring.

Doc with son John, who now lives in Preston and is a practicing physician in Harmony, Minnesota. Photo courtesy of Dr. John Nehring.

The Amherst store as it was in the 1960s and as it is today.

A mug shot of
A. H. Langum, justice
of the peace.

"The Last Man" in the
jailhouse smoking a
Kool and waiting for
a cup of coffee. Note
the baby shoes on the
radiator.

FBI wanted poster of Gil La Fountaine.

The former Fillmore County jail renovated and open for business as a bed and breakfast, the Jailhouse Inn. Photograph courtesy of Peter Guttman.

May Baskets

Hanging May baskets is a longtime tradition throughout Fillmore County. As I remember the tradition of hanging May baskets, it was for elementary-school children from grades 1 through 4. A boy would hang a May basket of assorted candies on a girl's door, knock, then wait for the girl to chase him. While serving as sheriff I experienced a couple of different variations of this tradition.

Starlight provided enough illumination for us to see a few feet ahead. A herd of beef cows thundered through the valley. The deputy and I walked with care along a steep wooded ridge, deep in the hill country, searching in the near darkness, for whatever was spooking the cattle. Already they had run through several fences and were spooked again, now by an indescribable wail echoing and bouncing across the valley between the bluffs.

Lawrence, a square-shouldered, heavy-set farmer, bow-legged with a wobble in his walk, had called us to the scene, dismayed by the eerie sound that continued to stampede his cattle in the darkness. We made our way back to the farmhouse where Lawrence's nineteen-year-old son, Phil, waited for us.

"What do you think it is, Sheriff?" Lawrence asked.

The disturbance had been going on for nearly an hour. Just then we sighted a shadowy figure moving along the wooded area near the house. The deputy and I gave chase, our flashlights extending our view in the darkness. We caught the figure making his way over a barbed-wire fence and marched him to our car's headlights to have a look.

"Why, that's my boy," Lawrence said.

"Bruce! What are you doing?" Phil asked.

"May basket," Bruce said.

"May basket?" I questioned.

It took a lot of explaining and was difficult to fathom even after the explanation. Bruce had just arrived home on furlough from the army and wanted to surprise his father and brother with a May basket. He'd been in the woods yelling "MAY BASKET!" at the top of his lungs. Bruce had kept repeating the call, waiting for the traditional chase—which never came until the deputy and I caught him. His holler had reverberated and echoed through the valley, making it indecipherable, driving the cattle wild. There was peace in the valley now except for the bawling of the cows trying to locate their calves. Why Bruce kept on with the caper after the cattle first stampeded, I will never know.

On another occasion in a rural setting in one of the more beautiful sections of Fillmore County, consisting of hundreds of acres of woodland, steep bluffs, crystal rivers, and fertile bottom land, Chester, a young lad of nineteen, went May basketing.

Two years out of high school, rather shy and immature when it came to girls, Chester heard rumors that Jill, a certain high school junior, rather liked boys. On the first of May, near dusk, never having had the opportunity to get acquainted with Jill, he parked his car a quarter mile from her country home. Leaving the back door of his car open, he placed one May basket on the trunk of his car and another in the back seat then walked toward Jill's house.

"MAY BASKET!" he yelled from the roadside, scarcely out of

sight of the house. Jill advanced inquisitively from her doorway down the steps. Chester retreated toward his car.

"MAY BASKET!" he repeated.

Jill trotted down the road to the car. Chester was hidden, slouched down in front of the grill.

"May basket," he intoned rather quietly.

Jill garnered the basket off the trunk, looked through the open car door, and reached for the basket in the back seat.

"MAY BASKET!" Chester said, pouncing on Jill, wrestling her into the seat, where shortly an intimate encounter took place.

Jill's mother appeared on the scene at a very inopportune or opportune time, depending on the point of view. But charges were filed against "Chester the May basketer," Jill being under the age of consent at the time. Chester received a sentence of three years. He served his time on probation under conditions of good behavior and completed his probationary period without further incident.

The Dead Guy

At 10:00 P.M. I picked up Doc Nehring at his house. A caller had reported a car off the road at a T intersection. A man behind the wheel appeared to be dead. There were no other passengers. We would be the first and only officers on the scene. As I drove, Doc hummed his little tune and asked one of the standard questions I had grown accustomed to.

"What do you think of me, Neil? Am I a pretty good guy?"

"You're an asshole, Doc," I said. A standard reply.

"Ho, ho, ho. I really like you, Neil."

On the rest of the trip, Doc, as usual, talked mostly about money and women.

"Turn on your red lights and siren, Neil," he said as we approached the accident scene. "Then when I get out everybody will be looking at me." I turned on the lights and siren for Doc. As I pulled to a stop I noticed something unusual in the headlights. Rather than the regular morbid expressions and people staring at their own feet, people were looking up with big smiles on their faces. Doc didn't notice. He alighted from the car, basking in the attention.

"Where's the dead guy?" he asked.

"He just ran in the woods, Doc," one of the onlookers said. Apparently when the first beams of our red lights flashed across the scene from a half mile away, the driver of the vehicle revived and decided a ditched car was no place to be.

I ran a vehicle registration check on the car. It turned out to belong to Dakota Wilson, one of our regular clients, accustomed to a bit of heavy drinking.

On the way back home Doc sang his little tune, "Humm hum hmmm hmm humm." He had a familiar look in his eye. "Say, Neil, I stopped off at the bar this one time I was up in Mille Lacs fishing. I was just sitting there having my drink, acting non-chal-ant. This bim sat down beside me and she bumped my leg. What was I to do, Neil? Hmm hum hmm hmm hmmm."

"Oh God, Doc, I don't know," I said. You never knew what was coming with Doc, but it was always something. "What did you do?"

"Humm humm humm humm . . . I bumped her back."

The next day Dakota stopped in to see Doc and got his broken nose straightened out. "Humm, hum, humm, hum."

Smile, Ed

Ed Ronald had hanged himself in an oak tree with a strand of baling wire. Doc Nehring, the Beson twins, boys about sixteen who had found Ed, and five other neighbors gathered around the tree with us. I knew Ed well. His son was a classmate of one of my brothers. I saw tears in the Beson boys' eyes, and the neighbors were looking down, quiet, with their hands in their pockets, shuffling their feet. Doc brought everyone to his attention with that serious speech of his that I'd become used to, about how he was the coroner and it was his duty to determine the cause of death. He told them, "It looks like a suicide, but I have to do a complete and thorough investigation." He fetched a battered old Kodak camera from his bag and paused, while looking around to make sure he had everyone's attention. Doc hummed his little tune, aimed the lens at the deceased, and in a loud voice said, "Smile, Ed." CLICK. Two weeks later he mailed me a copy of the picture. "SMILE" was printed in blue ink on the bottom border.

Say "Ah"

Doc and I stood in the haymow of a barn. The mid-July day was quite warm. I had just cut down a man who had hanged himself with a hay rope. He stretched across the hay, the rope still secure around his neck. Dr. Nehring took charge.

"I suppose everyone here thinks this is a suicide," Doc said in his most official tones. About a dozen of the man's neighbors gathered around us. Doc made sure he had their serious attention. "I'm the one that has to put the cause of death on the certificate. Can't assume anything. A very thorough examination is required."

I'd shared enough calls with Doc Nehring to know something was up. Doc fumbled around in his black bag that he always carried with him. An eerie quiet surrounded us in the barn.

"Humm humm humm hmm," Doc hummed as he brought forth a shiny scalpel. "Say 'Ah,' Barney," Doc told the corpse and cut the rope around the man's neck. The man had been dead for nearly two days. With the rope around his neck, gas had built up in his body.

"Ahhhh," said the dead man when Doc cut the rope. Everyone in the crowd jumped backward. Doc never looked up.

"Dum te dum dum dum," he hummed as he began going through the man's pockets, taking inventory.

Jesse James and Ernest Hemingway

The faded yellow house, its weathered paint cracked and peeling, sat far back on the lot next to a small Methodist church in the town of about five hundred people and four additional churches. The wide front porch was nearly obscured by bushes grown tall with neglect and the lawn was ready for haying. I parted the greenery of the bushes, made my way up the front steps, and knocked on the door.

"Harrumph," I heard from within, which for expediency I interpreted to mean "Come in." I opened the door and entered a kitchen, sparsely furnished but surprisingly clean and orderly.

"In here," a voice I deemed to be male said. I proceeded to an archway leading from the corner of the kitchen to another room where I thought the voice had come from. My mission was to apprehend the man and have him in court for a mental hearing at two that afternoon. It was 10:00 A.M. now. I hadn't gotten many particulars on the guy other than he was kind of a nut and forty-five years old.

I stepped through the archway.

"Far enough," said a man standing near the far end of the room with his back to the wall. I didn't heed his advice and walked a few steps farther. The man, about five-foot-ten, wearing a long black waistcoat, a white shirt, and brown tweed trousers, crouched slightly, with his wrists bent back at an angle near his hips, and spread his fingers wide apart.

"I'm Jesse James," he said. "When I count three we draw and shoot." His eyes were steely and I noticed a bulge in his waistcoat near his right hip. I stopped my advance.

"Damn," I said to myself. "I've done it again, gotten careless and got myself in big trouble."

"Wait a minute," I said, while mentally kicking myself for not even remembering his first name. "I don't have a weapon." (I didn't.) "I'll have to go get one if we're going to have a shoot-out." I turned toward the archway.

"Don't move or I draw," the man said and began parting his waistcoat with his right hand. I knew I couldn't make it to the archway if he had a gun. I was in the middle of the room with no place to go but perhaps to my grave. I decided the closer I could get to him the better off I'd be. I was six feet from him when he drew. I managed to grab his wrist before he fired from the twelve-inch green candle he'd pulled from his pants pocket. Jesse and I got on quite well on the way to the jailhouse, where I put him away to wait his hearing. Helen and I were polishing off the last of the Swedish meatballs and gravy from our noon meal when a knock on the dumbwaiter summoned me to the jail, where, by now, Jesse had transformed himself into a seafarer. He'd stopped up the floor drain in the washroom and turned on the water faucets. The sink was overflowing and he leaned on a mop handle swaying to the wash of imaginary waves in a stormy sea.

"Avast ye lubbers, man the mainsail," he commanded. I found it necessary to place the old sailor in a private cell, without plumbing, pending his hearing.

Later that afternoon, after leaving my man, who had reverted to being Jesse again, at the Rochester State Hospital, I decided I deserved a bit of stress relief. I chose the Pinnacle Room of the Kahler Hotel, which overlooked the Mayo Medical Complex and Rochester's southwestern horizon, for my relaxation.

A sheriff's duties bring him in contact with many characters, and some of his colleagues are a match for even the most unique of them. One of these, Willis Fraier, the sheriff of Dodge County, a snoose-chewing, whiskey-drinking curmudgeon's curmudgeon, called to me as I entered the Pinnacle Room.

"Neil, come on over. Sit down—I'll buy you a drink," Willis intoned in a voice tarnished by drink. He sat, slouched, in a corner booth accompanied by a white-bearded companion. They both appeared to have been imbibing for some time. I slid into the booth beside Willis, across from the bearded man.

"Shake hands with my friend Ernie," Willis said.

"Pleased to meet you, Ernie, I'm Neil Haugerud," I said, extending my hand across the table. There was surprising strength in Ernie's hand, but his voice was weak and words were slurred as he repeated my name.

"I met Ernie here at lunch," Willis said. I glanced at the clock behind the bar. It was five o'clock. I had my drink and found the conversation at a level that would have made more sense, perhaps, if I'd been drinking with the boys since noon. Willis asked if I knew where there might be some women, and Ernie seemed to be talking to himself as well as me about trout fishing. I had a second drink and listened for another twenty minutes, during which time, in order to make conversation, I asked, "What's your last name, Ernie?"

"Hemingway," he said.

"Ya, right, Ernie," I replied.

How fitting for my day, I thought. I bring Jesse James to the state hospital and have happy hour with Ernest Hemingway. It gave me a chuckle as I bade my colleague and newfound friend good-bye.

The following day after dinner, in the comfort of our living room, I scanned the evening paper while simultaneously watching television. My attention became more focused on the paper when I saw an article with a picture that resembled Ernie, Willis's friend.

The article explained that Ernest Hemingway was being cared for at Saint Mary's Hospital in Rochester and had been observed downtown occasionally when excused from care.

This story took place in early May 1961. Ernest Hemingway was admitted to Mayo and reportedly hospitalized and treated for depression at Saint Mary's Hospital in Rochester on April 25, 1961. He took his own life at Ketchum, Idaho, on July 2, 1961.

There's an area in eastern Fillmore County long shrouded in mystery and intrigue, a bit reminiscent of the Ozarks or the Kentucky hills. It's known as "The Big Woods."

Cal Meck, the game warden, didn't want to go poking around in the Big Woods alone. He had a report of someone shooting wood ducks out of season and asked me to go with him to investigate.

Sure enough, when we arrived at the suspects' isolated country homestead, there were duck feathers blowing about near a trash barrel in the yard. Our arrival was announced by the baying of a Black and Tan coon hound, straining at the end of an eight-foot length of chain where he'd trampled the earth bare and brown in a semicircle in front of his shelter. A couple of hybrid vehicles—part tractor, part car, and part pickup truck, ready for skidding logs, road hunting, or just going to town for a beer—were parked near the two-story frame house, its exterior paint long since weathered away. When I knocked on the screen door a gray-haired, stout lady, with greasy hands and wearing a soiled apron, welcomed us into the kitchen. The windows were all open, but the wood-burning stove overcame the west breeze and added to the oppressive August heat. Two bearded men in their early thirties sat at the table ready for the noon meal. Potatoes were boiling in a pot on the stove.

"My boys have been in the woods bringing up wood for the winter," the woman said, nodding to the men. "Whets their appetite."

"Did you boys shoot any wood ducks when you were down by the river?" the game warden asked.

"My boys are good boys," the woman replied.

The boys just looked at each other. The woman drained the water from the potatoes, put them in a white dish with a brown crack along one side, set them on the table, and went about making gravy in a fry pan. The pleasant aroma of roast duck seeped from inside the oven past the oven door and wafted throughout the room. I stood up, walked over to the stove, put one hand on the handle of the oven door and with the other pointed to the frying pan. I opened the oven door just a crack, then closed it. The boys leaned forward in their chairs ... wide-eyed.

"You know, Ma'am," I said, "that gravy'd be a heap better with some hot duck drippin's in it." I paused, savored the silence and the stares from the boys, then walked back to the entryway. Cal followed me to the doorway, then turned and faced the boys.

"Be sure you boys get a hunting license this fall," he said. "I'll be by to check on you." Both Cal and I knew that our presence had made our statement. We felt anything further would be counter-productive. For this wasn't any ordinary place; not at all. We were smack dab in the middle of the Big Woods.

The Big Woods is a unique cultural and geographic area, encompassing more than sixteen thousand acres of steep hills, bluffs, deep valleys, winding creeks, and the south fork of the Root River. The land, mostly hardwood forest, is interspersed with cleared acreage and intermittent productive farms. Located in mideastern Fillmore County, it's bordered on the south by the town of Newburg, on the west by Lenora, and on the northwest by Amherst. Populations in the towns were from two to twenty, and in the 1950s and 1960s Amherst and Newburg each had a country store. The area was settled by many squatters, some of whom lived in homemade tar-paper shacks or small trailers parked on land near a road with a clearing large enough for a garden. The squatters never bothered to find out who owned the land. Because it was in the back woods and only the timber had value, most landowners never bothered with the squatters. They lived mostly off the land. Deer, ducks, rabbits, squirrels, pheasants, and fish in the streams were taken without concern for fish and game regulations. Fox, raccoon, muskrat, and mink were hunted or trapped when pelts were prime. In the Big Woods there was no such thing as trespassing. For those willing and able there were plenty of jobs available working for local timber men. Over the years, many of the Big Woods young people married within the community, and whole families rarely left the immediate area. One or two small, well-hidden stills provided enough moonshine for the true natives. The homemade brew was not shared with the outside world.

The Big Woods people never presented me with any significant problems during my sheriff days, although some state officials had difficulty understanding the situation. State parole officer Tom Richards was in this category. Tom came to my office once or twice a month, often to pass the time of day, engage me in a few games of cribbage, and pick up on news of his parolees. He was a dedicated officer, an affable gentleman with a hearty laugh.

One mild November day Tom huffed into my office. His face was flushed, and he didn't look as if he was in the mood for a game of cribbage.

"Casper White's jumped parole," he said. "He doesn't report in, and I'm going to return him to prison."

"Casper's down in the Big Woods, Tom," I said. "I don't want to go down in there and try to dig him out unless he's stealing again. The Big Woods people are clannish. I need to be on the good side of them, so that if something real serious happens I have their support."

"I can't let him get by with not reporting in. What will I tell my superiors?"

"Casper's not a bad guy. Just a small-time thief. His dad Herman lives in the Woods. I could go talk to him and see if we could work a deal with Casper."

"I'm not working any deal. I've been in this business over twenty years and nobody has jumped parole on me yet and got away with it."

"But you haven't had anybody in the Big Woods, Tom. They've got their own code there. Now why don't you relax, we'll play a few games of cribbage, you go back to Winona, and I'll call you next week after I've talked to Casper's dad."

Tom reluctantly agreed. Then he beat me three out of five games of cribbage. Afterward he didn't seem so uptight. Two days later I had business in Canton and made my way home via the Big Woods and stopped at Herman White's place in a remote area along a dirt road. He lived in a small trailer at the base of a wooded hill with a south slope. His yard was strewn with old gas cans, paint pails, and junk parts. Two junked cars, the back half of a Farmall tractor, and the front runners for a sleigh were a few yards west of the house. An eight-point buck deer hung in a tree near a makeshift chicken coop. I didn't bother to see if it was tagged. Two dirty-faced little children parted a pair of dirty curtains on a dirty window and peered my way. Herman White came from the house to meet me as I alighted from my car.

"Whaddaya want?" Herman asked, his arms folded across his chest.

"Nice buck," I said, pointing to the deer.

"Ain't mine," Herman said.

"I was wondering if I could get a message to Casper?"

"Haven't seen 'im in weeks."

"If you do see him, let him know his parole officer is looking for him. Now as far as I'm concerned we can leave that situation to him and his parole officer. What's important to me is that we don't have any thievery in the surrounding area. You know, like missing pigs, chickens, and the like . . . you know like used to happen before Casper went to prison."

"My boy don't steal."

"Then you'll want to make sure nobody else in the Woods is stealin'. Anyway, you see if you can get the message to Casper." I walked to the side of my car and opened the door. Herman pulled a plug of Red Man tobacco from the upper pocket of his bib overalls and offered me a chew. I declined, but thanked him for the offer.

"Nice buck," I said again. Herman grinned and I drove away.

Tom Richards made a couple of futile attempts to apprehend Casper. Casper came in to Canton for a beer on occasion, but we didn't bother him and there was peace in the Big Woods.

Today, in the late 1990s, the Big Woods is attracting a new kind of fugitive. It began with a couple of escapees from academia. Then escapees from the urban environment began moving in. The latest escapee is from the multimillion-dollar corporate success world. That's okay, but I personally liked it better when there were more "Beware the Dog" signs posted than the "No Hunting or Trespassing" signs that the new fugitives display like wallpaper.

Casper still lives peacefully near one of the small towns bordering the Big Woods.

Humpty Dumpty

A golden harvest moon rested on the southeast horizon like a pumpkin on a porch rail as I sat half asleep, in my favorite reclining chair, the evening paper in my lap. My serenity was interrupted by a scream. Nothing raises the hair on the back of my neck like little girls screaming—and screaming little girls is what I heard, their feet thundering as they ran from the sheriff's office through the kitchen.

"Eeey! Eeey! Eeey!" they screamed, racing into the living room where I sat. I hurled my paper aside.

"Humpty Dumpty!" Renee exclaimed.

"Ya, Neil!" Mary Gross, the neighbor girl, sputtered. "Humpty Dumpty!" Susan was with them, too, and they all shrieked again, jumping up and down in delirium.

"What's going on here?" I asked grumpily. I didn't like my serenity disturbed for nothing.

"Humpty Dumpty's up in the jail!" Renee said. "He wasn't there Monday!" The girls, out of breath with excitement, began jabbering at each other and at me—all at the same time, of course.

"One at a time. One at a time," I said, holding my hands up for quiet. "What's with this Humpty Dumpty stuff?"

"We stick our fingers under the jail door," Susan replied.

"And then one of us raps on the door," Renee said.

"Then the prisoners grab our fingers," Mary said. The girls began jumping up and down again. "Oooooh!" they howled.

"We can tell who it is by the way they grab our fingers," Renee said. "Irvin is real soft. Tommy Wilson's fingers are kind of rough, but when Humpty Dumpty is in, his hands are always cold and he grabs real hard and sometimes won't let go! Today we didn't know he was in and he got Mary!" What next around this place? I thought.

"How long have you kids been doing this kind of thing?" I asked with concern.

"Oh, a long time now," Susan replied. "At first we'd ask who was pulling our fingers and they would tell us. Now we guess and they tell us if we're right."

"Ya!" They all chimed in. "Eeey! Eeey! Eeey!" They danced with excitement.

"Humpty Dumpty was first in way last winter," Mary said. "He scared us real bad then when he pulled so hard and told us he was Humpty Dumpty. And, and, and now he got us again. We didn't know he was there."

Humpty Dumpty—alias Pee Wee Hampton, alias Newton Hampton—had been in my office earlier that morning. He had signed a written confession to a burglary, after a half hour of inter-rogation. Afterward I had a strange feeling, one I'd never had after taking a confession. Pee Wee knew particulars only the burglar could know—but still, I wasn't sure I believed him. This wasn't the first confession I'd taken from Pee Wee. The first time, over a year ago, I'd roused him out of bed at 6:00 A.M. His wife, Ann, pulled the covers up around her neck. They lived on Main Street in a neighboring town, in a second-floor apartment above the hardware store.

Pee Wee asked, "Can I wash up before you take me down to the station?"

"Okay," I said and stood by the bathroom door while he washed.

Ann began to cry. "He hasn't done anything!" she shouted. I didn't respond. When Pee Wee came from the bathroom, we went down to the city police station where I questioned him.

Someone had burglarized a restaurant on Main Street. The burglar had broken the restaurant's basement window and made entry through a coal bin. After nearly an hour and a half of questioning I'd given up on getting anything out of Pee Wee, so I stood up ready to close the book on this part of the investigation. While washing up that morning Pee Wee had rinsed his head and combed a perfect part in his dark brown hair. Standing ready to take him home, I saw a black speck on the white of his scalp, in the part. What the hell, I thought, try anything. I placed a clean sheet of note paper on the table and told Pee Wee to give me his comb, stand up, and bend his head over the paper. Pee Wee complied, and I combed through his hair near the speck. Three minute specks, like pepper, appeared on the white paper. Putting my finger on one of the specks I made a black streak across the paper.

"That's coal from the basement of the restaurant," I said. "The crime bureau will be able to make a match with the coal. It's all over, Pee Wee," I said.

Humpty Dumpty had a great fall.

He spit out a confession of the restaurant burglary along with three recent additional burglaries in the area.

I only charged him with one of the burglaries, understanding the court would take the others into consideration after a presentence investigation. He was a first-time felon, and the court gave him probation. Now, a year later, here he was again.

Not wanting to spoil the girls' sport, I just grumbled, "You kids behave yourselves now." The next day Pee Wee recanted his most recent confession—not at all unusual for a burglar to do. I'm sure I could have had his probation revoked on the strength of the confession alone. But I felt something was wrong, so I took Pee Wee to a lie detector in Minneapolis where he passed with flying colors. Interrogation was my specialty and I was good at it, and it scared the hell out of me to believe that anyone might convince a person to confess to a crime he didn't commit.

As it turned out Pee Wee had a bad hangover when I brought him in. He was having marital problems. The court had awarded his wife custody of their children and placed a restraining order on him. In his mental state, apparently he felt he'd be better off in prison.

I later arrested the real burglar.

Domestic abuse, violence and threats of domestic violence were always frightening calls to respond to—not only frightening, but requiring communication and decision-making skills for immediate on-the-spot action. These calls were often life-threatening—never funny, but at times so absurd as to appear comical.

A pickax, its handle pointing at a sixty-degree angle toward a single light bulb on the end of a drop cord in the ceiling, was embedded in a four-foot-high mound of rubble in the middle of the kitchen floor. The kitchen, in a house without running water, was devoid of furniture other than an overturned table and four chairs. I'd driven twenty miles in a downpour in response to a woman's frantic call in fear of her husband. It wasn't my first visit to their place.

"What the hell's going on, Slade?" I asked. Slade, the husband, was camped on a stool with his legs braced across the top of a five-gallon crock that contained the household drinking water.

"The old lady accused me of having booze in the car," Slade said. The "old lady," wearing a lavender print housedress, stood near the wall opposite Slade with her arms folded defiantly across the front of her chest.

"He went out there to his car about every fifteen minutes and came back smelling of booze," she snarled.

"Now look what he's done." She pointed at the debris in the pile. It was the dangdest conglomeration of odds and ends I'd ever seen. An antique wooden toolbox, a carpenter's apron, an old pair of overshoes, a three-foot level, the back seat cushion and back seat rest from a car, a trowel, an old jacket, a huge pipe wrench, a pair of double-thumbed mittens, two hand saws, a miter box, an electric saw and drill, three feet of binder canvas, a short-handled spade, a spare tire and a jack, an old hat, a keg of nails one-quarter full, a wire stretcher, and I can't remember what else—all capped off like a grain shock with a pair of tire chains on top.

"Just get him out of here," his wife said.

Slade's overshoes, with remnants of dry cow manure on them, dripped mustard-colored liquid into the drinking water.

"Damn it, Neil," Slade shouted. "After she accused me of having booze in the car, I just went out and stripped that car of everything. To prove her wrong I brought it all in here and plopped it on the floor. I was more'n a little blistered. The last thing I brought in was that pickax, and I just sunk it into the top of the pile."

"He threatened to sink it into me before he put it in the pile," Slade's wife added.

"All I said was, there, you old bitch, that's everything from the car. Do you see any booze?"

It was obvious Slade had been doing some heavy drinking, and I'd gone through these kinds of discussions with them on previous calls. I knew I wouldn't get any rest if I didn't take Slade in.

"Well, Slade," I said, "you better come and sleep at my place tonight."

"At least I'll get some Goddamn breakfast in the morning that way," he said, and we walked to my car together.

Slade was known far and wide for his telling of tall tales, and he shared several with me on the way to jail.

"Neil," he said finally as we entered the city limits of Preston. "I think you might have to call Doc Nehring for me when we get to jail. My back is none too good. Last night, you know, when I was out doin' chores after dark, there was this hog trough mired in the mud so I picked it up and moved it to high ground. I thought it was mighty heavy, but I laid it to the mud. My back gave out just before I set it down. It was only then I noticed this three-hundred-pound sow, layin' sound asleep, in the end of the trough." The next morning Slade's wife decided against preferring charges and he was released.

Months later at breakfast downtown I was visiting with a cousin of Slade's who knew of the situation.

"You know where the booze was, don't you, Neil?" he said.

"No."

"Well," the cousin said. "Slade had put a long hose on the windshield washer and fed it back in under the dashboard. He filled the windshield washer container with whiskey. That way he was able to reach under the dash for the hose and get a drink any time he wanted."

I instantly awoke from the midst of a recurring nightmare in which I'm falling in space, my heart thudding in my ears between rings of the telephone. A bedside phone, although an irritant, was much better than stumbling to the hallway or downstairs at all hours of the night for who knows what odd reason. But I was jumpy, and this furious clanging within reach of my hand almost brought me to my feet.

I hadn't yet recovered from the previous night's call, when I'd attempted to prevent a suicide.

"Neil, this is Frank Rogers," the caller had said.

"Ya, Frank, what is it?" I'd replied. Frank was a young man who drank too much and lived a little on the wild side. I'd known him for some time now. He'd been in jail for his part in a brawl a few weeks ago.

"Call Doc Nehring and Dale Thauwald, bring them down with you to pick up the body," Frank said. "I've got a gun to my head and I'm going to shoot myself. I just called to say good-bye, Neil."

"Wait a minute, Frank." I began elbowing Helen awake. Thankfully she woke up on the second poke and I shushed her with my finger across my lips.

"It's no use, you're not going to talk me out of it," Frank said.

"Well, if you're going to do it anyway, there's no hurry then. Give me time to wake up a bit here and you can wish me a proper good-bye." I put my hand over the mouthpiece and told Helen what was happening. She should call Wayne, the deputy who lived next door; he'd know what to do.

I was able to keep Frank on the phone for about twenty minutes. I used every ounce of persuasion and every bit of expertise I could possibly muster, attempting to talk him out of it.

"We've talked long enough, Neil," Frank said with a definite tone of finality in his voice. "Thanks for the times you've tried to help me." I heard a click then, like a firing pin on a shell, and the sound of the phone falling to the floor. "Damn, it didn't work," Frank muttered like he was a distance from the phone. I heard something akin to a scuffle across the line, then Wayne came on the phone. He and Lee Tienter were at the house. They had just looked in the window when Frank pulled the trigger with the gun to his head, then rushed in when it appeared he was going to reload. When they examined the gun they found the firing pin had marked the bullet, but it was a faulty shell and hadn't gone off.

Now I had to shake off my apprehension before I brought myself to say "Hello." I looked at the clock. Last night's call had also been at two-thirty in the morning. The female voice on the other end was hesitant and apologetic.

"My name is Mrs. Forester. I'm sorry to bother you at this time of night," she said. "Is this where I call to report something I think is unusual?" I relaxed a little now, sure this wasn't an emergency call.

"If it can't wait till morning," I said.

"Oh, I'm sorry, but we ... my husband and I just moved to town, and I'm home alone. He went back to Minneapolis for the rest of our stuff. I probably shouldn't have called."

I sat up on the edge of the bed, puzzled by the polite apologetic manner of the caller. I'd had calls like this before from people not used to being home alone, frightened in the middle of the night. I tried not to sound annoyed or unconcerned.

"What's concerning you?" I asked.

"Well, our house is across the alley, behind the grocery store on Main Street. I got up after I thought I heard a noise a while ago and looked out our upstairs bedroom window. There's a ladder in the alley leading up to the second-story window on the store building. A light-colored car with an unusual shape keeps circling the block and coming through the alley, then stops by the back door of the store. There's no streetlight but I can see by moonlight. I think I saw the back door open, someone stepped out from the inside, and then two people went in. I thought it must be the owner, but the car circling around seems strange. It's probably nothing, but I thought I should call you."

I was alert now. This was far more than unusual. "Stay on the phone!" I said loudly.

Helen usually slept through anything. Many times I'd take a call in the middle of the night, be out for hours, return, and she'd never know I was gone until she'd ask at the breakfast table if there had been any calls. When she was about ten she slept through a chimney fire at her house and didn't wake up even when three firemen paraded through her bedroom. But if one of our children whimpered at night, even two bedrooms away, she'd be up in a flash.

I was able to elbow her awake now and handed her the phone.

"Keep this lady on the phone while I get dressed," I said and bounded out of bed. I put on a pair of trousers, ran downstairs to the office, and used another line to call Lee Tienter, the town cop, at his home. Lee woke quickly and said he'd be in his car within minutes. I switched to the other line where Helen was talking to Mrs. Forester. "The car just went through the alley again," she said. "I think there are two men in the store. I can't see too clearly." I broke in on the conversation.

"Mrs. Forester," I said, "please stay on the line until Helen comes downstairs to the office. It may take her several minutes. She'll have to get some clothes on first. Okay, Mrs. Forester?"

"Yes. I'll hold on."

I ran upstairs, and by the time I was finished dressing Helen had her robe on and was in the office on the phone with Mrs. Forester again.

I grabbed a rifle from the gun cabinet and headed for my car. Gartner's Grocery was three blocks from the office. Lee was in his car, on the radio, when I backed out of the driveway. I told him to check the front of the store, and I'd drive in the alley.

Helen called on the radio. She said Mrs. Forester saw my car when I drove in the alley. The odd-shaped car had pulled away several minutes before, she said. She thought someone was still in the store but she wasn't sure. Lee called on his radio and said cardboard boxes were piled high in front of the store windows so he couldn't see inside. The front doors were securely locked, so Lee came around back with me. Neither of us felt at all good about stepping inside that door, but we did. The door led into a rather dark storage area, then into the main store where the lights were on. Lee ventured forth in one of the grocery aisles, I in another; we paused to listen. We didn't hear anything. I scurried to another aisle and looked about. There was a second level above to the rear. I ran ahead to where I could get a view. Lee proceeded to another aisle where he could get a look at the safe. The door was wide open, the dial was off, and it was cleaned out.

"Be careful, Neil," Lee said loudly. "The safe's been busted." Warily we searched the area. With all the grocery aisles, storage areas, meat-cutting rooms, and partitions, it was difficult and dangerous work. We were lucky. The burglars were gone.

It was a professional job. The inside of the safe had been pushed out using tremendous force on the dial shaft. After we were quite sure there was no one in the building we called the owner. Lee stayed at the store until the owner came down, while I went back to the office and notified area law enforcement agencies of the burglary. The description of the car was too incomplete, I thought. Even so, Floyd Mohawk, Chatfield's policeman, might be of some help. He was a legend, a warehouse of information. He'd come to Chatfield in 1932 as part of a construction crew building a new highway through town. Floyd participated, quite successfully, in many of the amateur boxing matches that were sponsored in the area at the time. He was appointed special policeman in 1939 to tame down some of the local toughs causing fights and disturbances in the taverns. He did so in short order. Floyd, a mild-mannered, swarthy man of few words, with a small black mustache and a slow, deep bass voice, later became Chatfield's full-time police officer, one of the best officers in the area. When cars were cruising around that he didn't recognize (which seldom happened because he made a point of knowing the make and model of every local car), he jotted down the description and license number on a notepad he carried with him. Floyd spent most of his time on foot patrol and often appeared seemingly out of nowhere when least expected. His only uniform was a black leather jacket.

On a hunch I thought I'd check with Floyd. He might give me something even with a description this vague. He answered on the third ring when I called.

"Say, Floyd," I said, "there's been a burglary here in Preston. Gartner's Grocery. A safe job. A woman from behind the store observed a car driving through the alley about the time it happened. All she knows is that it was a light-colored car shaped somewhat different than the ordinary."

"Oh, Neil," Floyd drawled in slow, deep words, as if they were dragged from the bottom of a bass drum. "That's a 1960 Ford Thunderbird, New York license plate number NY 5654." I never said "Are you sure?" to Floyd Mohawk. His word was gospel.

"When did you last see it, Floyd?" I asked.

"I made a trek through the alleys just before one. I saw it then. I was on foot, but then I got in my car and cruised so they'd know I was around. They left town heading south."

"Thanks, Floyd. You're a great help," I said. "I'll get back to you later. I need to get this information on the air. Thanks again."

"Okay, Neil," he said, and hung up.

The description and license number were on the air within seconds.

Lee and the deputy were dusting for fingerprints at the store when the first rays of sunlight lit up the eastern sky.

The state patrol radio crackled in the sheriff's office.

"Rochester patrol to Fillmore sheriff."

"Fillmore sheriff, go ahead," I replied.

"Car 18 has observed the Thunderbird with New York plate NY 5654 approaching Mississippi River bridge to La Crosse, Wisconsin. It would be difficult to stop in Minnesota. Advise."

"Ten-four, Rochester. See if he can keep the car in sight. I'll contact the La Crosse sheriff and police department to assist when they cross the state line."

"Ten-four. I'll notify our car and be right back to you."

The La Crosse police spotted the car when it came across the bridge. We decided to make the stop when the car reached the outer city limits, where the sheriff's patrol was stationed for assistance. But the car turned off the highway into downtown La Crosse and stopped at the hotel. Three men carrying luggage, a potato sack, and a large shopping bag entered and registered for one room. They were taken by a bellman to room 414 on the fourth floor. When the bellman came back down on the elevator he was met by four uniformed police officers who ushered him back up to room 414. On instructions from the officers, the bellman knocked on the door. "Bellman," he said. "I have extra towels for you." The door opened, and the four officers, with guns drawn, rushed into the room.

"Up against the wall," they commanded. One of the men reached for the bedspread, which had been pulled back across the bed, then thought better of it when two of the policemen's guns centered on his head.

One of the officers lifted the bedspread. Underneath were cash, checks, and three .38 caliber revolvers.

"Careful, men," he admonished, "get the cuffs on them."

The first thing I did when I got the report that the suspects were safely behind bars in La Crosse was to call Floyd Mohawk, thank him, and give him all the credit he deserved.

But the case wasn't over yet. The suspects were tight-lipped in Wisconsin. They did, however, waive their rights to an extradition hearing, and we returned them to Minnesota and the Fillmore County jail. As I requested, they had been isolated from each other while incarcerated in La Crosse. In our jail there were only two secure areas, so necessarily two of them were housed in the same compound. After we brought them to Preston they were questioned by agents from the FBI and the Minnesota Bureau of Criminal Apprehension. They refused to answer any questions. Maybe that softened them up. Anyhow, I gave them a try after the other agents left. One by one they confessed and gave signed statements admitting to the Gartner's Grocery burglary and two more burglaries in a neighboring county.

When we received their FBI records we found we were dealing with two experienced, potentially dangerous criminals and a young accomplice without a record.

Tony's record listed pages of previous burglaries, as well as an arrest for distributing narcotics in Greenwich Village using a vegetable pushcart as a cover.

Richard's record covered several pages of felonies plus a stint in Guatemala as a mercenary, as well as an escape from the maximum security prison at Huntsville, Texas.

Henry's record was clean; he was the apprentice son of a butcher in the Bronx.

After they pleaded guilty they were sentenced by the court. Henry was given five years and released on probation. Tony and Richard each received a sentence of ten years in prison, Tony at Stillwater and Richard at Saint Cloud because of his younger age.

I received another wake-up call for my carelessness around the jail when I took Richard to Saint Cloud.

"Sheriff," he said as the gray stone walls of the prison loomed on the horizon, "you've got to be more careful or you are going to die a very young man." By now I'd come to know Richard quite well, and there was no animosity between us. "You would have been a dead man in any other jail I've been in," he continued. "Only one thing saved your life. Your family. Other places I've been, cops were just cops, screws were screws, and nobody gave a shit. But your little girls played games outside the doors with the prisoners. We saw them playing in the yard with you and their friends. We heard you and your wife talking and playing with the kids in the house. Any other place I'd have snuffed you. I had more than one chance. You need to be more careful, Sheriff. The next guy might not notice your family or give a damn. Another thing, if you'd've been in that grocery store ten minutes sooner, when Tony and I were in there, there would've been big trouble; we had guns and we had the advantage. It's not worth the risks you take, Sheriff."

Richard's admonition became even more significant three weeks later, when he escaped from prison. He was the second person ever to scale the wall of the Saint Cloud reformatory.

Tony was from New York and never received visitors, so I stopped to see him whenever I brought another prisoner to Stillwater. On my third visit, he said to me in his Italian accent, "Sheriff, ya-s gotta stop-a da comin' ta see me. I getta da bad name up here."

A Naughty Lady

My days at the jailhouse were often exceedingly hectic. At times days and nights seemed to run together without end. Often it took great resolve to keep my cool. So when the phone rang at 5:45 one foggy morning, after I'd been in bed only two hours, rather than answer the irritant I wanted to smother it with my pillow. But I answered, and within twenty minutes I was at the scene of a car accident where two people had been killed and a young girl severely injured. By ten o'clock, when I arrived back at the office, the telephone was ringing, the two-way radio was chattering, and someone was pounding on the jail door. The deputy answered the phone, and I grabbed the keys and went up to the jail.

"That guy waiting for court is getting kind of wild," an inmate said as I unlocked the door. He was referring to Reggie Fields, a strapping twenty-nine-year-old with a history of mental illness. When we'd picked him up the previous day he'd smashed his furniture with a sledgehammer and was just about to demolish the television set. Reggie was screaming obscenities at me as I unlocked his cell door and entered.

"Calm down, Reggie," I said. I was going to say more, but Reggie fixed a glassy stare at me and the next thing I knew he had both hands on my throat, trying to push my Adam's apple out the back of my neck with his thumbs. I was getting rather short of breath by the time I yanked his hands off my neck, whereupon he grabbed each side of my shirt collar and ripped my shirt off. This seemed to satisfy his need to let off steam, and he calmed down. I told him I'd bring his dinner up to him and we'd be going to court shortly after that. The change in Reggie was swift and amazing. We sat down on the bunk and visited like old friends. Reggie seemed utterly unaware that any altercation had taken place. His court appearance was at 1:30 P.M. After the hearing I delivered him to the state hospital in Rochester.

When I returned to the office two hours later, the phone was ringing. The state patrol and the sheriff's radio networks were directing messages our way. I was about to speak to a farmer who had been waiting to see me about cattle missing from his pasture when Helen popped into the office asking where the groceries were that I'd promised to get for the prisoners' supper.

"Oh ya. I just forgot," I said. "I've got the list right here in my pocket. I'll get them as soon as I'm through here." I filed the report about the cattle and told the man I'd see him at his farm the next morning. My car was out front, and as I bounded down the steps to the sidewalk en route to get the groceries, I met a businessman coming to the office with a complaint about a worthless check. I said, "Talk to the deputy in the office," and got into my car. I reached for the ignition and the shifting lever, but they were gone—so was the steering wheel, the foot-feed, and the brake pedal. Startled, I looked around. In my haste, I'd gotten into the back seat. The businessman stood staring at me with a puzzled expression. I felt my face flush red and pretended to be looking for something in the seat before getting out, sliding into the front seat, and driving away.

When I came back with the groceries I told Helen I'd had it with all the commotion of the past few days and wanted to get away for a bit.

"I'm going fishing and won't be back till after dark," I said.

I drove to the Fillmore Township area, one of the most scenic areas in the county, and didn't stop until I was at the end of an abandoned township road in a green wooded valley. I radioed in and told the deputy I'd be out of service for a few hours. After retrieving my fishing pole and tackle box from the trunk, I walked down a dry wash gully toward the river, turning over stones in wet areas in search of night crawlers. The gully was narrow and cool, now and then canopied by treetops. As I walked, my mind quieted and my sense of awareness began to change. Deep in the wooded valley I became conscious of something unusual. At first it seemed as if I might have lost my hearing. There was no sound of traffic, ringing telephones, radios, horns honking, human voices, or other noise that usually cluttered my everyday life. In the mystifying silence I stopped and sat on the trunk of a fallen elm that bridged the gully, where lime-green ferns and bright wildflowers grew, avoiding the sun. I cleared my mind and consciously listened. Out of the calm I heard the slight rustling of leaves in a gentle breeze. A nearby cardinal whistled a call and received an answer from across the valley. A blue jay scolded a chattering squirrel. I sat quietly, looking and listening as the valley came alive with the songs of other bright-colored songbirds.

"Thump thump thump ... thump thump thump thump," a grouse drummed. Its miniature thunders, created by flapping its wings faster than the speed of sound, echoed through the valley. A frog trilled its musical chimes. Crickets chirped all about me. A rooster pheasant crowed in the distance. The enticing sound of gurgling water in the river riffles beckoned me onward.

A racy animal smell wafted through the air as I approached the river. My mind's eye pictured a red fox marking the boundaries of his territory. At the riverbank, I baited my hook with a night crawler, cast my line into a deep pool, and sat down. I found a native mint leaf at my side, crushed it between my thumb and forefinger, and inhaled its fragrance through appreciative nostrils. I leaned back from the riverbank contentedly listening to the chorus of the woodland, while eyeing a red-tailed hawk circling above in a patch of lonely cloudless sky.

I couldn't entice the smallmouth bass with night crawlers so I cast a few lures, without success. With only a half hour remaining before dark, it was time to pull out all the stops. I tied my only Naughty Lady, a black-and-gold feathered lure about the size of a dragonfly, to the end of my line and cast it into the rapids. As soon as it hit the water a huge bass inhaled it from the surface and ran upstream, stripping line from my reel. I managed to turn him around, but he took another run for the rapids, leaped into the air, shook his head, and slapped the rushing water with his tail. My line went slack; the bass and my lure were gone. I felt I could go home now, for darkness was setting in and this was no place for me to be without a Naughty Lady.

There were fourteen towns in the county, ranging in population from 185 to about 1,800. Each town had at least one justice of the peace. They dispensed justice as good as that found in the district courts with robed judges and formal procedures, only they did it more openly, with more color and flavor. No need for side-bars in justice court.

A. H. Langum, the justice in Preston, was a crusty and opinionated retired county newspaper man about eighty years old. He held court in a musty cubicle in the basement of the post office building, which he owned and rented to the government.

"How do you plead?" Judge Langum asked the defendant who had been brought to his court by the state game warden for fishing out of season. A stringer of trout lay on the floor by the desk.

"Not guilty," said the defendant.

Judge Langum rose. Color came to his face. "What do you mean, not guilty," he demanded indignantly, pointing at the floor, "when there lay the fish!"

In another case, Cyrus Blagsvedt took the stand in Judge Langum's court. Cyrus, sixty-some, with a three-day growth of rusty beard on his ruddy face, wore a wrinkled plaid shirt, khaki pants, and high-topped work shoes. His dark hair was wet and shaggy, and he held a brown cap in his hand. Cyrus was one of those men who always has a pleasant look on his face. Even today, with his right eye swollen and purple-black around the edges and blood where the white of his eye was supposed to be, he looked pleasant enough. Being the complainant, he was ready to tell his story. I had charged the defendant, Jack Irons, with petty larceny: stealing gas from Cyrus's gas barrel on the farm. Jack sat in the corner of the musty basement with his young lawyer, who was just out of law school and about to begin his real education.

"What happened to your eye, Cyrus?" Judge Langum asked curiously. Cyrus was Norwegian. He didn't speak English until after third grade. "Vell ... ah ... yer honor. It don't haf anyting to doo vit da case. Ya know. Sir yer honor."

"I'll decide that," the judge said indignantly. "Tell the court what happened to your eye."

"Vell, your honor. I'm from out in da country, ya know. By da Big Voods ve, ah, ah ... don't talk like you town folks, ve swear a little, ya know. I tink I better not."

"You tell the court in your own words what happened to that eye!" the judge demanded.

Cyrus looked at me. "Neil. Vy don't you tell dem. You know vot happened. I can't explain like you city folks, ya know."

"I'm running this court," said the judge. "Now you tell the court or you'll be held in contempt."

Cyrus looked down at his shoes and cleared his throat. "Ahem. Ahem." He looked up at the judge pleadingly. "Vell, your honor, it vas yesterday. I vas on my farm minding my own business getting ready to go to da sawmill, when dat Got damn Leonard McCabe came by. He vas vit dem bastards ven day stole de gas, ya know. Da son-uf-a-bitch vas drinking. I guess I took a little nip from his bottle, too, ya know. Anyvay dat asshole Leonard, he yumped into the truck vit me and rode along to da sawmill. All da vay along he vas telling me I had ta drop da charges on dis here gas stealing. He yust kep' on and on. And on da vay back I finally called da son-uf-a-bitch a suck-ass and he hit me in da eye. Right der in da truck."

The case was all downhill from there.

His eyes were never vacant, but Joe Petty, Spring Valley's justice of the peace, never looked straight at anyone—for good reason. A blow to the head, by someone using brass knuckles during a fracas in his home state of Montana, resulted in permanent nerve damage, which caused his right eye to be fixed, staring at the bridge of his nose. Later Joe migrated to Minnesota, a trip that included spending a few months hiding out on the Rosebud Indian Reservation in South Dakota. Joe was a "little big man": five feet two, 130 pounds wringing wet, thin-limbed and tough as rawhide, with a face the texture of dried prunes. "A nimble cat," one of the town cops said, when describing him.

Joe dispensed justice in a ten-by-twelve-foot cinder block city building, which contained a holding cell, a desk, and a few folding chairs. It was a dark and musty place, with only one small window on the east wall and a single light bulb in the ceiling. Traffic violations, disorderly conduct, petty theft, and minor assaults constituted most of the cases heard in justice court. Joe, even though he always looked like he'd just come in off the prairie, made a point of wearing a white shirt and string tie for court, which he conducted in a dignified and efficient manner. His paperwork, which was required to be filed at the courthouse, was always in precise order. Justice was meted out as judiciously and fairly as any court in the county, including district court.

Joe was employed by one of the iron mining companies. Performing duties as a justice was only an occasional, part-time, task for justices of the peace throughout the county. Spring Valley was the business hub of the iron ore mining industry in the area and a tough miners' town—especially on Friday and Saturday nights.

"Just what is it Joe does?" I asked my friend Jerry, one of the town policemen, over coffee one day. "He always seems to be available for court during the day." Jerry chuckled.

"Among other things, I think he does some late night core sampling on farm property where the farmers don't really care for the mining companies to be core sampling. Kind of a prospector, like he was out west," Jerry said.

"That must be hard work, alone in the dark."

"He's not averse to using dynamite to assist in the gathering of samples. We get an inquiry now and again from farmers wondering what the loud noise was that woke them up during the night. I asked Joe about it once. 'Sonic boom,' he said."

We could use others, but I liked to use Joe as a justice. It took a little while, but once Joe began to trust us he became a great resource, a treasure trove of information on every owlhoot that lived within fifty miles.

Joe gave nearly everyone we dealt with a nickname. Violet Sommers was tabbed "Pissy Sommers." Pissy was an older, grungy lady who frequented the bars. When going from bar to bar she'd often stop before crossing the street, spread her legs, and urinate straight down to the curb.

"Pisses more than she drinks," Joe said. We brought Violet before his court on a bum check charge on a hot summer day. The small enclosure was not well ventilated and Violet had an aversion to soap and water—the odor was far from pleasant. I stood in the open doorway, but Joe couldn't escape the stench. He fined her ten dollars. She didn't have the money. Joe was smart enough to know we didn't want her in our jail so he gave her sixty days to pay.

"Goddamn," he said, rushing through the doorway for air after Pissy left. "That woman smelled like two barrels of shit boiled down to a pailful and strained through a skunk's ass."

"Gumfoot" was Joe's name for the part-time town policeman who thought of himself as a great detective. He often came to Joe seeking a warrant on some misdemeanor charge without a shred of evidence.

"The Cougar," as Joe called him, spoke in a deep gravelly voice that began with a unique stutter and ended with a quick flurry of words. He was a huge, strong man, six-foot-six or more, who drank considerably but seldom became obnoxious.

"Where you been, Coug?" my friend Jerry asked one day.

"Bbbee be be bbbeen been spending nights in Marchant's used car motel," the Cougar replied.

"You can't be sleeping in those cars," Jerry said, and made arrangements for him to get a cheap room at the hotel. Cougar received a disability pension from the army, and from what we knew, he didn't stutter or drink before he went to war. Rumor was he'd been blown up on a bridge in Germany.

Because of his stutter he was often the brunt of a good amount of teasing, some of it downright mean. One day in the pool hall he'd had enough. Without saying a word and before his antagonist could make a move, the Cougar's huge hands had him by the lapels of his coat and lifted him off the floor. He hung him by the back of his coat collar on a wooden peg in the wall so his feet didn't touch the floor.

"Do do don don don't anybody go near him till I say so," the Cougar said. And nobody dared. If I'm not mistaken I think that was the day Joe named him "The Cougar."

I had the Cougar in jail a couple of times for being drunk and took him to the Willmar State Hospital once. We got along fine. But a terrible thing happened a few years after I was sheriff. The Cougar killed his mother with a hammer, and he later died in prison.

Tilly Overton, a spindly, wrinkled old woman, who wore black and carried a black umbrella, spied her way around the courthouse square of the town of Preston each morning, purveying and seeking tidbits of information and gossip.

One morning Doc Nehring, visiting with Bill, the undertaker, at his furniture store–funeral parlor, watched her birding her way along the street pecking seeds of gossip from each passerby.

"Bill, here comes Tilly," Doc said. "Let's play a trick on her. I'll get on the slab in the embalming room. You cover me up with a sheet."

Tilly always stopped by to inquire of Bill on the well-being of the local citizenry. By the time Tilly toddled in, Bill had busied himself among the furniture. Her ankle-length black dress billowed from her hips and swished the furniture as she edged her way through the aisles toward him.

"Good morning, Mr. Heitner." Tilly's voice scraped across her vocal chords like an overworked reed on a clarinet. "Did anyone take a walk with the Lord last night?" Bill folded his hands, lowered his head, and spoke in his somber undertaker's voice.

"Poor old Doc Nehring passed away," he said. Tilly plucked a black hankie from the pocket of her dress.

"Oh, that's so sad," she said remorsefully, dabbing

at her eyes with the hankie. "Could I have a last look at him?" she asked.

"I guess that would be all right," Bill said. "He's out back." He ushered Tilly to the slab in the embalming room and reverently removed the sheet from Doc's face. Tilly looked at the doctor, clutched her umbrella in folded hands, and stood in silent prayer for a moment.

"I expect in many ways he may have been a good man," she creaked. "But I knew that drinking and carousing throughout the night would bring him to an early grave."

Doc's belly, suppressing laughter, began to shake. Just in time, he raised his arms to ward off the blows to his head from Tilly's umbrella. Bill was laughing so hard he was no help at all.

Helen often mentioned she'd like to have an older home to remodel some day, one we'd live in when I was no longer sheriff or after they built a new jail, whichever came first. When I became sheriff, we used money from the sale of our house and business to buy a farm in the hills and woodlands next to the Amherst store. The property, we thought, would keep pace with inflation until it came time for us to purchase a home again. The farm had nearly one hundred acres of woodland and a rundown house without electricity or running water. Amherst, twelve miles east of Preston, on the edge of the Big Woods, consisted of one of the last of the oldtime country stores and Lilly's house. Lilly, the store's proprietor, a diminutive, craggy-faced woman of considerable character and widow of an alcoholic husband, had of necessity kept the place in its original decor.

We often spent part of our weekends on the farm. One Saturday, I took Renee, Susan, and Mary Gross, the neighbors' girl, to the farm, where powder puffs of clouds glided across a deep blue sky sending their shadows scampering along the landscape of green pasture land and fields of gold August grain stubble. We did a few chores before our traditional Lilly lunch, a meal the girls said was "just the best."

Lilly purchased from her vendors only what she could pay for in cash; often her grocery counters were sparsely stocked. Clifford, her Pure Oil gas man, who drank intoxicants only once a year, and then steadily for about thirty days, wanted to fill the thousand-gallon underground tank as long as he had made the trip from town.

"I only got fifty-seven dollars for gas today," Lilly said bluntly.

"That's okay, Lilly," Clifford said. "I'll fill it up. You can charge the rest." Lilly huffed a coarse breath.

"I ain't chargin' nothin'. Put in fifty-seven dollars' worth or don't put in nothin'." Lilly wiped the back of her hand across the outline of a black mustache above her upper lip.

"But Lilly, you can pay me later, no interest," Clifford said. Lilly, ignoring Clifford, walked behind the meat cooler out of his sight. Clifford went outside and came back shortly.

"Fifty-seven dollars, Lilly," he said. Lilly counted out the money from an old cash register sitting among a clutter of weekly newspapers and grocery sacks, on a service counter with a lemon-colored linoleum top.

A farmer brought some canned goods and three loaves of bread to the counter.

"You can't take three loaves of bread," she said. "You have to leave some for the others. Come back Thursday. I get a new order in then."

A kerosene stove, with a stovepipe extending through the top of the east wall, heated the building. Two faded lime-green stuffed chairs with threadbare arms and a beige couch with gray stuffing protruding from the cushions sat in the vicinity of the stove to facilitate social gatherings. We ate our Lilly lunches here when it was cold outside. Today we planned to have a picnic on our farm. I picked up a box of Saltine crackers from the double shelves that ran the length of the store. Lilly squinted at the girls with a hint of a smile.

"What kind of pop do you girls want?" she asked.

"Strawberry."

"Grape."

"Root beer."

"Neil?"

"Root beer," I said.

"I suppose you want some Thuringer and longhorn cheese, too," Lilly said as she pushed a few strands of long gray hair away from her eyes. Her voice was high-pitched and salty as if it had aged in an oak cask. When she asked a question, which was often, she expected an answer, now.

"Just figure out about how much we need for four, Lilly," I replied.

She was wearing the same gray apron she'd worn the last few times I'd been there. She brought a round of Hormel Thuringer and a brick of longhorn cheese from the cooler, placed it on a plywood cutting board on the counter, then wiped a huge knife on her apron.

"About this much, Neil?" she asked, placing the blade on the Thuringer before she looked to the girls. "I suppose you girls want yours cut up in slices. Neil, he always just takes a big chunk. Where's Helen today?"

"She had to feed the prisoners," Renee replied.

"I s'pose they gotta eat, too. Damn fools." Lilly finished cutting the meat and cheese, wrapped it in wax paper, and tied it with a string. The pop, a local brand whose recipe dated back to 1897, came in old-fashioned bottles. Lilly retreated through a gray chipped door by the heater to the back room, where her late husband had worked as a mechanic, and came back with a box for our groceries. "You want the caps off this pop?" she asked.

"No, we're going to the woods for lunch," I said.

Today these girls, now in their forties, will say that those lunches with Saltine crackers, Hormel Thuringer, longhorn cheese, and Spring Grove pop were the best they ever had. And as this is written Lilly still has the store at Amherst.

We had a fine picnic in a cedar grove on a hill above the store and returned to Preston.

There were no calls during the night, and I woke up early to a fine Sunday morning. Our bedroom faced south, with two tall windows that looked across the alley toward the Root River. You couldn't see the river from the window, but above the houses you could follow its winding course by the willows, oaks, and elms that grew along it, as clearly as if it were drawn on a map. Steep bluffs rose above the treetops on the far side of the river.

I heard a squawking shortly after I arose. Across the alley, Freda, our neighbor, was plucking chickens and depositing the white feathers in a fifty-five-gallon burning barrel. A bloodied butcher knife, a pail of steaming water, and the roosters' severed heads were at her feet. A southwest breeze, moist and already warm, stirred through the windows. Anticipating a quiet, relaxing day, I put on a pair of khaki pants and a white T-shirt and went downstairs.

I was at the kitchen table drinking coffee and reading the Sunday paper when the phone rang. A frantic woman, Marcia, whose husband I'd dealt with before, needed help right away. There were no police in the small town where they lived, five miles away. Lute, her estranged husband, was going to kill her. They'd argued; he was on his way to get an ax so he could do the job right. I knew Lute could be dangerous. I hollered up the open stairway to Helen and told her I was going on a call and would be back shortly, and was on my way.

Lute, dressed in a brown suit, white shirt, and tie as if he were ready for church, was approaching the house from about thirty feet away when I stepped from the car.

"Watch out! He's got a knife!" Marcia shouted from inside the screen door. Lute continued to proceed toward the house, a menacing look on his face. I ran between him and the front door.

"You got a knife on you, Lute?" I asked, forcing a calm voice.

Lute pulled open his suit coat with his right hand. Eight inches of butcher knife, gleaming in the sunlight, protruded from his inside coat pocket.

"You Goddamn right," he growled, "and I'm going to use it, too." A mental picture of blood all over my white T-shirt flickered across my mind. My blood.

"Lute," I said, outwardly composed. "I want you to do some serious thinking. You're not in any big trouble yet and there's no good reason for you to get in trouble, trust me." I moved as close to Lute as I could without being threatening. "I think it would be better if I had that knife." I kept a close watch on his eyes; they lost some of their steely glare. Very gingerly I reached inside his coat and removed the knife. He didn't resist. I felt a lot better now.

"You don't have anything else on you, do you, Lute?" I asked.

"Nope, nothing," Lute replied, but flashed a menacing stare at Marcia.

I began a routine pat-down. I felt a large hard object inside his shirt, just above his belt line in front. Lute, thankfully, was as docile as I'd ever seen him; he'd given me some trouble the last time I picked him up for being drunk and disorderly. I pulled his shirttails out of his trousers. A wicked, razor-sharp hatchet extended above his belt, the handle extending down inside his pant leg. I was frightened when I removed it—the hatchet head was level with my face before the long handle was completely free of Lute's trousers. Marcia began to say something. I interrupted. "I think it would be better right now if Lute and I drove down to Preston and tried to get this straightened out," I said. The last thing I needed was an argument to break out between Marcia and Lute while that ax and butcher knife were still in the vicinity.

"Let's get out of here, Lute," I said. I motioned him to the right front seat of the car. After he got in I locked the ax and butcher knife in the trunk.

It was near lunchtime when I'd finished the investigation and had Lute locked up in the downstairs bull pen awaiting justice court on Monday morning.

I had nearly finished lunch and was reading the Sunday paper when the phone rang again.

"This is Mrs. Weston Rootwell," a hysterical woman cried across the phone line. "Weston's going to kill me and the kids. Do you know where we live? Get here right away."

"Yes, Fillmore Township, right?"

"Yes."

"Where's Weston?"

"He's outside right now. I don't dare talk any longer." The phone went dead.

I told Helen I had to go on another call and asked her to leave the door to the office open again so if I needed anything she would hear the radio.

"What is it this time?" she asked.

"Oh, just a family squabble," I told her and thought, Oh shit, not another one of these. I hope my luck holds.

When responding to a potentially dangerous call, it's easy to let your mind conjure up all sorts of scary scenarios. Enough so that by the time you get to your destination you're almost too frightened to proceed. I'd learned to divert my thoughts. In addition to the task at hand, something else was usually going on inside my mind. When I pulled into the Rootwells' driveway my mind was playing piano, a rendition from one of our girls' recitals. The rendition was interrupted by the crack of a high-powered rifle shot. I surveyed the farmstead with quick glances in every direction. A man carrying a telescopic rifle ran from near the barn and entered a cornfield some fifty yards north of the house. I parked at the end of the drive and ran to the house. With every step my mind pictured my head in the scope of that rifle. I kept moving diagonally to the corn rows, knowing the seven-foot-high corn would prevent anyone from getting off a good shot. A frightened woman met me on the porch. Her three young daughters were with her. There was no time for introductions or explanations.

"Stay right here," I said. "I'll pull my car up across the sidewalk next to the doorway. When I stop all of you get in the car as fast as you can." The woman shouted something after me that I couldn't understand as I ran to the car. When I skidded to a stop after my front wheels had crossed the sidewalk, my mind made a picture of the back of my head in that scope again. The woman and the three terrified children piled into the car and we sped from the scene. I drove northeast toward Chatfield. The woman identified herself as Vivian Rootwell. As we drove Vivian told me that her husband, Weston, had been very abusive lately. She had bruises on her arms and face as evidence.

"This morning he said he was going to kill all of us," Vivian said. "He pushed me up against the wall and put the rifle barrel under my chin." There was an ugly bruise on her chin where the rifle barrel had been. "He said not for any of us to even think about trying to make a run for it. 'It will only make it more sporting for me to pick you off on the run,' he said." Vivian sobbed, at times unable to talk. The girls huddled together in the back seat.

"Then he went outside with the gun," Vivian continued, "and set up a target on some bales of hay by the barn and began shooting. Then I heard him say, 'Take that, you bitch.' I was scared to death when I called you. I'm sure he never thought I would dare, but I was more scared for the children than myself. Thank God you got here."

I got the family a room at the Chatfield Hotel. After getting them settled in their room, I notified Floyd Mohawk, Chatfield's policeman, and gave him a description of the green Pontiac I had seen at the farmstead. Floyd said he would keep on the alert and make sure the Rootwells were safe. I drove back to the Rootwell farm and finished the piano recital on the way. The green Pontiac I'd seen in the yard was no longer there. Vivian had assured me that there was no one else at the farm so I assumed Weston had taken the car. I drove back to Chatfield and further interviewed the Rootwell family. I knew they would be okay with Floyd checking on them so I drove back to my office, where I obtained the license number and description of the Pontiac. I put the information out on a statewide all-points bulletin for the apprehension of Weston Rootwell.

That same day, Jim Knight and his wife, Kim, good friends of ours with whom we regularly socialized, came by our house for cake and coffee at four. Kim, who is Japanese, married Jim when they met in Tokyo while Jim served in the U.S. Army. She thoroughly enjoyed cooking and took great pleasure in Jim's appetite for her culinary creations. I chuckled to myself as Kim described her first experience with Dr. Nehring. She told us a very amusing story about the house call when Dr. Nehring came to treat Jim for the mumps. Doc seemed as much interested in Jim's football coaching as he was in his illness, and before he left he questioned Kim at length about her ancestry and the Japanese decor of their home. He provided them with free medication and didn't charge for the house call.

Jim and Kim had stayed for supper and left at seven. At 9:50 P.M., I received a radio call from the Rochester sheriff's department reporting that they had apprehended Weston. He was drunk and had run off the road near Stewartville, eighteen miles west of Chatfield. He had a loaded deer rifle in the front seat of the car. Before I could respond regarding further disposition of the case, the phone rang again. A man spoke in a coarse whisper. I could barely discern his voice.

"This is Doug Ramstead at Club 16," he said. "Get down here right away. Rusty Johnson's here. He's got a gun, he points it over the bar and demands a beer for him and his ex-wife. He's threatening her. I got to go before he sees me at the phone. Hurry. I'm scared as hell." The phone went dead. My stomach contracted into a tight ball. I'd had enough of this for one day.

I had good reason to be scared. Rusty had interrupted my sleep with a call two weeks earlier saying he was going to kill me. He'd been drinking and was upset with me for taking his son to prison about a month earlier. I hadn't paid much attention to Rusty's call; I thought he was rather harmless. I wasn't so sure now.

I radioed the Rochester sheriff's office and asked them to hold Weston Rootwell overnight and I would check with them on Monday.

Thinking I could use some backup on the call to Club 16, I phoned Preston's policeman, Lee Tienter. Lee was extremely trustworthy and dependable in dangerous situations and often accompanied me on calls as a special deputy. I told him not to wear his uniform jacket. I'd begun to formulate a plan in my mind. We were on our way to Club 16 within minutes. I'd been on calls to the club before, a roughhouse tavern two miles west of Rushford. I pretty much knew the layout of the place—two entrances, a long bar, a small dance floor. We pulled into the parking area and parked where my car wouldn't be observed. We heard dance music and the normal revelry one might expect as we approached the building. We had decided Lee would post himself in the east entryway. I'd go in through the front door. A man fiddled a dance tune, accompanied by a woman playing piano, and the floor was crowded with dancers when I stepped inside. I shouldered my way through the crowd of standing beer drinkers. The bar stools were all occupied. I spotted Rusty on a stool; thankfully, he had both hands up on the bar and wasn't looking in my direction. I made my way through the crowd, grateful no one recognized me. I squeezed in behind Rusty and touched him on the back.

"Rusty," I said in a low voice right next to his ear. "If you as much as move one of your hands I'll knock you cold." He turned his head and looked at me with an icy stare. "I'd like for us to get outside for a talk without anyone getting hurt," I said.

Rusty drew his right arm back on the bar. I showed him the lead-lined leather sap I had in my hand. "Don't even think about it," I said. He stopped his arm movement. The fiddler finished his tune to a round of applause, then announced the next dance and began fiddling again. There wasn't anyone in the place that knew of the crisis other than me, Rusty's ex-wife, Ann, and Doug, the bartender, who had made himself very scarce.

"I understand you have a gun on you, Rusty," I said. "Now keep your hands where they are till I get it off you. Then we can discuss this further."

"I don't have any gun on me, Neil," Rusty said. His voice was reassuring and he turned his face to the bar.

"Fine, then we won't have any difficulty. I'll just pat you down."

"You don't have to do that." He was wearing bib overalls over another pair of trousers.

"Keep relaxed, Rusty," I said and began patting him down. I felt a hard object just above his belt line on his right side. I reached inside the overalls and withdrew a revolver tucked beneath his belt. I quickly pocketed it.

The band never missed a beat and the reveling continued uninterrupted. No one noticed us.

"Walk over to the side entrance," I said to Rusty. "We can talk outside." He obliged. When Lee met us in the entryway, a great sigh of relief escaped me and my knees grew weak. Outside Lee put the handcuffs on Rusty, and we put him in the back seat of my car. I took the gun from my pocket and unloaded it. It was a nine-shot .22 caliber, fully loaded. I put the bullets in my pocket and locked the revolver in the glove compartment. Lee stayed with Rusty while I went back in the club to talk to Doug and Ann. She said Rusty had put the gun in her ribs a couple of times and told her to keep her mouth shut. Doug said Rusty had pointed the tip of the barrel of the gun over the bar and said, "Give us each a beer and keep your mouth shut or else."

The fiddler was preparing for the next dance as I stepped

through the doorway on my way to the car. He drew his bow across the fiddle. "We start the next set with 'Heartaches by the Numbers,'" he announced.

It wasn't until we were back in Preston and Rusty was securely locked up with Lute that I sat down for a breather in my office and the last strains of the piano recital played in my mind again. I didn't even want to think of another day like this.

Lute got sixty days, fifteen of which he served in our jail. The remaining days were suspended for one year under conditions of good behavior.

Rusty received a sentence of one year in the county jail, of which he served thirty days. The remaining sentence was suspended for a period of two years on conditions of good behavior. Neither man ever caused any additional serious trouble.

Weston's case was something else again. He didn't have a previous record, and his wife, Vivian, declined to press charges. He had gone in the ditch in Olmsted County. All they charged him with was careless driving and having an encased gun in the car. He was fined one hundred dollars.

He had no previous record, but had called our office some six months earlier complaining about the unruliness of his fifteen-year-old daughter. She had begun to stay out past eleven at night without permission and was dating an eighteen-year-old boy. Some days later, when I happened to be in the area, I'd stopped by and talked to Weston and Vivian. Vivian had very little to say, and Weston was "concerned about his girls growing up in a permissive society, the way it had become." I had chalked it up to overly concerned parents and went on to other issues. Now in hindsight the call carries far more significance for me.

After extensive interviews with Vivian and two of her daughters, fifteen and thirteen, the young girls confided to me that their father had been forcing them to have intercourse with him for some time. The fifteen-year-old said her dad became enraged the first time he found out she had gone out with a boy from school.

In this rural area it was next to impossible in most cases to do anything about incest. The courts and the county attorney were reluctant to deal with it. The abused families refused to go public or give testimony, since everyone in the area knew them. As in this case, the wife and the children were too terrified to testify. Without their testimony we had no case. But other strange things had been going on in the area, like a series of cattle thefts. With six months of coordinated effort with the Rochester sheriff's office, we made a strong case for cattle theft against Weston Rootwell. We made sure his presentence investigation contained information of the incest. While he was in prison his wife and children escaped from his domination.

There was only one prisoner in jail and the sheriff's log noted only one morning call, a Rushford merchant complaining of a no-account check he'd received from Stub Peterson. Stub, an alcoholic whom I'd tried to help out a few times by giving him work and letting him stay in the house on my farm when he was down and out, had used me as a reference when he wrote the check.

It was a pleasant, sunny, and mild day for late November. Renee and Susan were at school. At lunchtime I helped Tom, now thirteen months old, into the antique highchair that had been his maternal grandmother's, and shared my mashed potatoes, gravy, and peas with him. Helen had an aura, a contented motherhood shine, about her. At the dinner table we concluded our plans for Thanksgiving; this year it wouldn't be the same. Traditionally we observed Thanksgiving at my parents' home, but this year would be the first without my mother. She had died of cancer on October 27. She was sixty-four. The family, thinking it would be nice for Dad if we all got together again, decided to carry on the tradition. With my sister supervising a cooperative effort, we were asked to bring scalloped corn and candied yams.

I told Helen how lovely she looked. She smiled and volunteered to put Tom to bed for his nap. His room at the top of the stairway was just across from our bedroom. As Tom was drifting off to sleep, Helen brought an armful of towels and washcloths from the kitchen laundry to the bathroom upstairs. We met in the hallway and kissed; what with one thing leading to another, as sometimes happens, you know, soon we found ourselves embracing in the bedroom.

"No," Helen said to my suggestion for further romance. "Don't even think about it. This place is like Grand Central Station. Someone will be at the door."

"The phone hasn't even rung since nine o'clock," I said.

"Something else will happen," she said.

"It's only a few days before Thanksgiving," I said, holding her close. "Nothing will happen. All is quiet on the western front." I pulled the covers back on the bed. Helen, who suffers from a phobia related to undressing in front of anyone, retreated to the walk-in closet. In short duration she reappeared in her housecoat.

"Never, ever again if something happens," she threatened, slipping into bed and pulling the sheet up around her neck.

"Nothing will happen," I assured her as I cuddled beside her.

And so began a romantic interlude. Suddenly the front door, at the base of our open stairway, burst open. We heard someone charge into the foyer.

"Neil, Neil!" my brother yelled from the bottom of the stairs. "The president's been shot. Kennedy's been shot!"

Invariably, at least once a year or so, when we are out socially someone poses the question, Do you remember where you were and what you were doing when Kennedy was shot? Helen blushes and turns away, then attempts to change the subject. Occasionally, at first, I'd tell on her. But you only need to use your imagination to perceive why I might have learned that this was not a good idea. You might also perceive the punishment I will receive when this is published.

I genuinely liked the Fraser boys. To this day I still have a soft spot in my heart for them and don't feel I would have led a full life without knowing them. They were basically honest little thieves, honest to their upbringing at least, and there wasn't a mean bone in their bodies. They wore a sense of humor on their faces, had a certain air of dignity about them, and never complained of their circumstances or made excuses for their actions. The blueprint of life set before them contained a number of social flaws for which they paid the price without flinching.

I first met Kent and Lyle Fraser when they were ten and eleven years old, respectively. They regularly spied on old Pop Henderson, who was batching it in a rather ramshackle two-story house on a small acreage a half mile from their home. Shortly after dark one evening Kent, with his brother Lyle on lookout, watched through a basement window as Pop deposited rolls of twenty-dollar bills into a mason jar and hid it behind jars of rhubarb sauce on the canned goods shelf. Years behind on support payments to his ex-wife, he refrained from depositing money in any bank out of fear she would somehow attach it.

A few days later, Pop called my office and reported that someone had entered his house while he was gone and had stolen twelve hundred dollars. He showed me down the stairs to his damp cellar. As I was nearly a head taller than Pop, my forehead forged a new path through the cobwebs hanging from the ceiling joist as we made our way across a well-trodden path in the dirt floor to the rickety wood shelving where he stored his canning. Blue-green mold grew on the lids of the peach jars and a thumb-sized, black-green lizard's tail protruded from beneath the moist rot of an oak board in the corner. Pop showed me where he had hidden the money.

"Whenever I got as much as five twenty-dollar bills, I'd roll them up and put a rubber band around them. Then I'd put 'em in a quart jar and hide 'em down here," Pop said. He brought a handful of rolled-up twenties, each bound with a rubber band, from his pocket. "I had two jars with twelve hundred dollars each in 'em. Half the money from each jar is gone. Could be my ex-wife's doing. She always said she was going to get half of everything." Pop looked up at me with questioning eyes, set in a spider web of worry lines.

I was puzzled as to who might take only half the money, but was convinced that an ex-wife with back support payments due wouldn't let a guilty conscience halt her theft in midstream. I considered the possibility of the culprit being one of Pop's drinking buddies, who'd be considerate enough to spare him some cash. But Pop said he'd more or less quit drinking and none of his old friends had been by in months. It must have been children, I thought, inexperienced at thievery at this level.

If the culprits were kids, I knew, given time, that they'd make some foolish mistakes. There was no sign of forced entry; however, the door locks were old, and any skeleton key could unlock them.

"I've got some ideas, Pop," I said. "In the meantime you better find a safe place for your money. Ever thought of a bank?" I chided. He put the rolls of twenties in his front pockets and led the way upstairs, his trousers hitched above the paunch of his stomach and his gray socks showing above his high-top shoes.

"I know what to do with the money," he said when he reached the top of the stairs.

"Let's just keep quiet about this for a couple of days while I do some checking around," I said. Pop nodded agreement.

The next day, without raising suspicion, I networked my contacts to determine what children between ten and sixteen years old lived in the locality. Most rural areas were so comfortably small that everyone was a neighbor or friend, and information of the type I sought was easily obtained. Proprietors of country stores were a wealth of information, so I made a practice of stopping by the stores in the county on a regular basis. Jake, the proprietor of the nearest store, an earthy guy with an earthy vocabulary, wasn't at all surprised by my visit. We first talked about the weather, fishing, and the lady who'd recently painted her white house in red and blue polka dots.

"Any kids unusually flush with money lately, Jake?" I asked.

"Not that I can think of," Jake replied. "Flush with money! Shit, ain't nuthin' but paupers and Free Methodists around here. Paupers don't have any money and Free Methodists don't spend any money. The way things are going I'll be closing the damn doors in a month or two." I selected two loaves of whole wheat bread to take home with me and placed them on the counter. Most rural folk don't especially appreciate or respond to direct questions immediately.

"Anything else?" Jake asked.

"That'll be it," I said. I paid for the bread and was walking out the door when Jake spoke up.

"Say," he said. "Lyle and Kent Fraser were in and bought a bunch of candy, not unusual I guess, but normally they have to scrape up all the change in their pockets to pay for it. Yesterday they paid with a twenty-dollar bill and got change back."

"Let's keep this information between ourselves for a few days, Jake," I said.

"You damn right, doubt if there will be anybody in to talk to anyway."

Kent and Lyle were already near the top of a suspect list I'd gotten from a contact, and the report on their mother was none too good, either. It would be best if I could intercept them away from home. Luckily while cruising the townsite I found the two boys about four blocks from home and invited them into my car. After a few questions and a few denials they told the whole story. Kent was a round-faced, round-bodied, little bandy-legged boy, smug and confident for his eleven years. Lyle was slim-featured, and pleasant-mannered, with darting blue eyes that looked Kent's way for direction before he spoke. I felt embarrassed and reluctant to talk to these little boys without their parents present. But I figured I would be doing them nothing but a big favor by thwarting their outlaw careers at the beginning of their errant ways.

They admitted to watching Pop when he hid the money, and, the next day, after seeing him drive away, letting themselves in his house with a skeleton key and taking his money.

"Where's the money now?" I asked. Kent wiped his fingers across his brow, then produced a twenty and some change from his pants pocket. Lyle tugged at the sleeves of his faded plaid shirt.

"We hid the rest in a coffee can near a culvert by Hank Ernik's place," Lyle said. They were friendly now and wanted to be helpful. I drove with the boys to the hiding place, where we retrieved the coffee can with the money, but there were only some six hundred and fifty dollars inside.

"Where in the world did you boys spend over five hundred dollars already?" I asked. They stared at each other momentarily. I could tell they shared a secret neither wanted to reveal.

"Don't tell," Kent admonished his younger brother. I'd begun to appreciate these boys and exercised patience with them; soon they told the story. They'd put the rolls of twenties in their pockets and walked home. When Kent took his hand from his pocket to open the front door, two of the rolls had fallen to the front steps without his noticing. Later their mother found the twenties on the steps and confronted the boys. They confessed they'd taken the money from Pop's house but hedged on the amount, telling her they'd taken only seven hundred dollars. Their mother demanded five hundred of the loot from the boys and later that day bought a new television set from the money she'd taken from them.

I had hoped the case could be handled informally through social services, but an order from the juvenile court judge would be needed before they could intervene and the county attorney declined to take a case against the mother.

Kent and Lyle, charged with delinquency, appeared before juvenile judge "Itch" Stanley, aptly nicknamed for his habit of continually scratching his genitals in public. Itch was a pretentious lawyer judge, learned in the law, as they say. After a short hearing, and well aware of the complaisant involvement of the boys' mother, who sat in court with them, he released the boys with a mild verbal reprimand and placed them on probation—to their mother!—provided Pop Henderson would be reimbursed for his full loss.

It was as if the court had just issued the boys a license to steal, and during the next eight years Kent and Lyle were regular customers of mine for thievery and burglary. They did time in two of Minnesota's state correctional facilities.

My idyllic view of the legal system, born both of innocence and ignorance, began its nonstop slide, to the point that in my mind high court justice, administered by black-robed intelligence, fell to a much lower level than the occasional, harmless uncultured fumblings of the justice-of-the peace courts.

Ginny and Bobbi

There wasn't a specific statute or city ordinance to cover Ginny's offense, so she was charged with being drunk and disorderly. While drinking beer with some of her town cronies in a tavern, an argument erupted over which milk tasted the best. Some insisted it was cow's milk. Others insisted it was goat's milk. Ginny insisted it was mare's milk. The argument became heated.

"I'll bet my slick ass none of you dead-pecker dirt farmers or city slickers have ever tasted mare's milk," Ginny said.

A man with a full beard, slobbering drunk, took a swallow of beer and licked at the foam in the hair above his lip. "Probably so thick it would stick and cake to my whiskers," he said.

"How about you, pig-eye," Ginny said to a wide-faced man with a patch over one eye, "ever drank mare's milk?"

"There was this ol' girl I went out with one time called 'old hoss.'"

"Don't try to be a smart asshole," Ginny interrupted. Then she stood up from the table, put on her buckskin jacket, and went outside. Within two minutes she burst through the front door astride the mare she'd ridden into town. It had been tied up in the alley. She dismounted and proceeded to hand milk the mare into a beer glass, which she then passed around for tasting.

The fat man with a veiny nose who ran the tavern, not taking kindly to the proceedings, came out from behind the bar and ordered Ginny and her horse out of his establishment. In turn, Ginny had a few choice words for the proprietor, who then called the cops. When the policemen came in the front door, Ginny led her mount out the back, overturning several tables in the process. A wild ride through the streets ensued. Ginny and her horse refused to stop for the flashing red lights of the pursuing city police car. After she got cornered in a blind alley, she kicked one officer in the face when he grabbed her arm and commanded her to dismount. Eventually the city police subdued Ginny and brought her to the county jail in handcuffs. She wore brown, hand-tooled cowboy boots, a buckskin jacket with fringes, a yellow shirt with a string tie, and trousers that fit tightly. She was weather-tanned, with shoulder-length blond hair and a pretty face. Her blue eyes below moon-shaped eyebrows became like dark holes when she looked at the officers. The officers took the cuffs off her and I booked her in; she was twenty-nine, five feet seven, about 120 pounds. The policemen had taken a hunting knife with a six-inch blade from her belt when they apprehended her. I found another knife, with a three-inch blade, tucked inside her boot. She was quite tipsy and had a scowl on her heart-shaped face.

"Well, Virginia," I said, using her given name, "are you ready to go up to your room?" Ginny stood up, swayed a bit, and glared at the officers who'd brought her in.

"Assholes," she said. I took Ginny by the arm and we walked toward the jail door. The two officers followed. Once inside the jail we took her up a flight of stairs to the bull pen. She sat down on the lower bunk and dropped her head and shoulders, her hands nearly touching the floor. I stood directly in front of her. I thought she might be nauseated and was thinking of getting her a pail to throw up in. Suddenly she straightened up, thrusting clasped hands at my midriff. Something made a pinging noise as I caught a blow to my stomach. I grabbed Ginny's wrists. One of her hands held a steel rat-tail comb. Luckily the steel tip had caught in my belt buckle or it would have punctured my stomach. I still don't know where she got that damn comb, but I nearly broke her wrist before she let go of it. It all happened in a flurry without a word spoken. I flipped Ginny onto the bunk, picked up the comb that had rattled to the floor, stepped away from the wild woman, and turned to the two policemen.

"Will you guys stay here and keep a watch on her while I go get a female to search her thoroughly? If she's got matches on her, she'll try to burn the place down."

"Are you nuts?" Helen asked. She was curled up on the couch in the living room. I'd made my request while interrupting her evening news program on TV. She asked what Ginny had done, and I toned down the story as much as I dared.

"You mean you want me to go up there and frisk that wild drunk woman who just tried to stab you?"

"There will be three of us right there," I said. "She's real subdued now; she thinks I broke her arm. All you have to do is see that she doesn't have any matches on her or anything she could set fire to the jail with."

"A half hour ago I was sitting in the rocking chair contentedly rocking our baby. That's more my style. I like babies. Get somebody else to search that woman."

"I don't know of anyone else. Come on, it will be hours if I have to find someone else."

"She'd probably smash me like a little bug," Helen said, waving me off. It took some smooth talking but I finally convinced her.

The Spring Valley officers and I stood by the cell door while Helen conducted the search. Ginny didn't give any further problem. "Hurry up and get this over with. I wouldn't even let my husband do this," she said to Helen.

It was over an hour later when I climbed into bed and snuggled up next to Helen. Her attitude was a little cool.

"Don't you ever ask me to do that again," she said. "I'm just not going to do it. Ish."

A few weeks later, the Spring Valley city fathers passed a special ordinance that said horses couldn't be in the city limits after sundown. Ginny and her sister Bobbi ignored it, of course, and were arrested. The city attorney, thinking the ordinance might be unconstitutional, dropped the charges after the two pleaded not guilty.

A few months later, Bobbi, a black-haired, broad-faced, muscular woman, a few years older and seventy pounds heavier than Ginny, threatened us with a shotgun when we served an eviction notice on Ginny and her. They hadn't paid the rent for a year and refused to leave.

Bobbi was rough and tough. She once threw a water glass at Wayne, the deputy, when he had a warrant and was looking for the culprit she shared a mobile home with. The water glass shattered on a doorjamb and cut his arm. A superficial cut—he ignored it and Bobbi.

Another time Bobbi was hospitalized while serving a jail sentence for disorderly conduct. When the doctor released her to go back to jail, she refused to leave her hospital bed. Wayne got the assignment to bring her in.

"Get the hell out of here, you son-of-a-bitch," was her greeting when Wayne entered her hospital room with two nurses.

"You've got five minutes to get ready," Wayne said. "I'll wait out in the hall." About three minutes later one of the nurses came out of the room.

"Bobbi took off her gown, threw it on the floor, got in bed naked, and covered up with a sheet," the nurse said. Wayne didn't waste any time. He pulled the door open and went into the room.

"Your choice," he said to Bobbi. "Get ready now or I wrap you in the sheet and take you the way you are."

"Screw you, ass-face," she said.

Wayne was six feet two and strong as an ox. In a matter of seconds he had Bobbi wrapped tightly in the sheet, but she'd managed to scratch him on the arms with her fingernails and draw a little blood. He was halfway to the door with Bobbi slung over his shoulder when she changed her mind.

"Okay, you bastard, I'll get ready and go with you," she said. He set her on the floor and pushed her against the wall.

"Five minutes," he said. Bobbi was back in jail within a half hour, a model prisoner.

Ginny spent another thirty days in jail for disorderly conduct in August 1964. Sober and in jail and she acted the perfect lady. I even let her out to help Helen with the housework on several occasions. They got along well and had a chuckle over their first meeting.

Another time Ginny was found unconscious by a passing motorist on the highway near her home on a cold fall night. Her horse stood nearby in the ditch. It appeared she had fallen from the horse and hit her head on the cement. The doctor called to the scene said she was near death and she was rushed to the emergency room at a Rochester hospital. As it turned out, Ginny had blacked out from an aneurysm while riding and had fallen from her horse and received a concussion. About a month later she was standing in her yard as I was driving by. I stopped to see how she was doing. As we stood in the yard chatting, her nine-year-old son came running from the house with a rifle in his hand.

"Here, Ma," he said, handing her the weapon, his little blue eyes glaring at me and the police car. Ginny cradled the rifle in her arm and patted the boy's head. "It's all right," she said. "This is Neil, the sheriff. He's okay."

The NFO and the Last Man

I left the door from the kitchen to the office open while we ate. My dad, Sherman, had stopped by about 5:30 and stayed for supper; he was drinking his third cup of coffee and smoking his umpteenth cork-tipped Kool. The kids had gone to the living room to watch TV when the office telephone interrupted the silence at the table. I'd never really talked to my dad. He'd talk to my wife, Helen, and one of his other daughters-in-law but hardly ever carried on a conversation with any of his ten children. Sherman was about five foot six, trim as rawhide and tougher than a boiled owl. He had the Democrat donkey logo with four stars above it imprinted on his bank checks along with the phrase "The Last Man." He could hardly wait for a Republican to ask him what "The Last Man" meant.

"I'll tell you what the Last Man is," he'd say. "It was in 1929; a few of us rented the town hall in Harmony. When the city fathers found out we were going to organize a county Democratic party they kicked us out, and we had to hold our meeting in the woods south of town and use oak stumps for chairs. I'm the last man alive who attended that meeting."

Now the Last Man followed me to the office and stood in the doorway while I spoke on the phone. The call was from a livestock trucker who'd had his windshield shot out. He laid it onto the NFO.

"They should shoot out all their damned windshields," Dad said loud enough to be heard over the phone. I grimaced and shook my head, feeling that a comment from me would be like pouring gas on a fire.

The National Farm Organization (NFO) had called a holding action to keep agricultural products off the market until an agreement on pricing was made with the buyers. Dad was a member and staunch supporter of the NFO and its holding action, which included efforts to keep nonmembers from selling their products. I told my dad I had to go and left him for Helen to take care of. She was good at it—smooth.

Since the beginning of the holding action our office had responded to several disruptive incidents. The driveway of a local livestock buyer had been blockaded. Keys were taken out of trucks, several truck tires were slashed, and sickle sections were placed on roadways in front of trucks, with the intent to cause blowouts. I pretty much knew who the NFO members with potential to cause problems were and knew that they were most active late at night. I often made a point of being in a patrol car, in uniform, parked in their farmyard when they came home at two, three, or four in the morning. I didn't have anything on them, but they didn't know that. They were farmers without experience participating in protests and boycotts, so my mere presence in their yard really got their attention, and incidents were infrequent in our area.

A situation with great potential for disaster took place when the regional NFO members announced that they were going to blockade the Lanesboro Sales Barn's weekly livestock auction. Members from Minnesota, Iowa, and Wisconsin were all to come in force to Lanesboro and prevent the Friday sale from occurring. I was informed that up to four hundred NFO members would be on hand to make good on the threat. A week before the sale, Walter Ode, one of the sales barn owners, called me.

"You're not going to let them stop the sale, are you, Neil?" he asked. Walter was a mild-mannered, reasonable sort of man; however, he was very concerned and agitated over the issue.

"I'll take care of the situation," I replied. I didn't have any idea what I'd do about the predicament. I was apprehensive, having no experience with these kinds of protests myself.

"I talked to the Lanesboro police and the fire department," Walter continued. "The fire chief said as soon as the NFO-ers try to stop a truck from unloading I should give him a call. He'd blow the fire whistle and all the volunteer firemen would come running and put a stop to things."

"Walter," I said, "if this is the way you want to handle it, okay by me, but I'll probably be at least a hundred miles from here."

"Then what do you recommend, Neil?"

"If you want me to handle it, just say so and I'll take care of it. If you want the fire department to handle it, I'm totally out of it."

"What will you do?"

"I'll have to make my decisions as the situation develops, and I'll need your promise of cooperation no matter what takes place."

"We can't have that sale shut down, Neil."

"If it means stopping bloodshed we might have to, Walter." There was a long pause. Walter cleared his throat about four times.

"We'll leave it up to you then, Neil," Walter concluded.

Two days before the sale I made my decision on strategy. I wanted to make sure no one got hurt or killed. There was potential for both.

I gave Ed Morine, the ag instructor from Spring Valley, a call. He was a good friend of mine and very handy with an 8mm camera (high tech for the times).

"How would you like to be a special deputy for a day?" I asked.

"What's up, Neil?" he responded, with a suspicious tone to his voice.

"Oh, a few hundred NFO members have vowed to stop the Lanesboro livestock auction on Friday. Rather than a show of force, which I don't have anyway, I was thinking it might be effective if you accompanied me with your movie camera and we'd get as much of the action on film as possible. It will be a deterrent to the farmers. Hopefully they'll believe we'll be able to identify them on film doing anything illegal. Rather than making arrests at the time we could use the pictures for identification and evidence to make arrests later when things have calmed down."

"But I'm well acquainted with a lot of the local members, Neil."

"All the better, Ed. I'll put my uniform on without a jacket and make sure everyone can see I don't have a weapon on me. All you have to do is run the camera." Ed was hesitant.

"That group from Wisconsin has gotten kind of mean lately, from what I've read in the paper," Ed said.

"Yeah, I know, but I've decided to shut the sale down myself if it looks like there will be any violence. They can always have another sale."

"Okay, I'll meet you at your office on Friday morning."

Ed and I were at the sales barn by 9:30 Friday morning. It was only five blocks from Main Street, near the Root River. A boisterous crowd had already gathered; we began taking pictures, panning each group. I was thankful the Last Man wasn't in the crowd. When the first livestock truck arrived to unload, more than three hundred protesters were assembled near the unloading area. One group stood seven or eight deep in front of the chute as the truck began backing to unload. Ed and I positioned ourselves close by and Ed began filming. The protesters didn't like that camera at all. They looked at Ed and me, then back to the truck, and then began to part; soon there was a clear path for the truck. Several protesters retrieved cameras from their cars and began taking pictures of Ed and me taking pictures. I thought this was a good sign; I was encouraged. Thereafter the sale continued, with different groups gathered here and there plotting strategy and one group always on hand to shout and curse at the truckers. A few members taunted Ed and me, but the day ended without further disruption.

About two weeks later at a similar protest in Bonduel, Wisconsin, two NFO members were killed when run down by a livestock truck.

I saw Walter Ode in Lanesboro about a month later.

"Neil, you did a good job," he said. "We're lucky nothing happened like it did in Bonduel. Boy, there were some tough-looking characters in that crowd we had here. I remember that one big burly guy with a black leather jacket shaking his finger in your face. He was a mean one."

I kind of laughed. "Walter," I said. "That was one of my men. I recruited five tough-looking special deputies and had them spread out in the crowd. That mean one was just reporting to me what was going on and where. He pointed out a group that he thought was most likely to cause trouble, so we went over and took their picture."

"Well, I'll be damned," Walter said.

The Last Man hadn't been to the jailhouse for a visit for some time. Helen asked about him one day when she knew I'd been to Harmony.

"Did you see your dad?" she said.

"Ya, I saw him in front of the post office."

"What did he have to say?"

"Nothing."

"You didn't talk to him? Were you across the street or something?"

"No, we passed on the street. I was going one way, he was going the other."

"And you didn't stop and talk?"

"No, but we said hello to each other as we passed."

It was only a couple of days later that he came by the jailhouse and stayed for the noon meal.

"I don't know what the hell you were doing with that guy and the camera down at Lanesboro," he said.

But he didn't fool me this time: a friend of mine had told me how he'd heard Sherman bragging to the boys at the coffee shop about the great job Neil had done at the sales barn in Lanesboro.

I sipped on a cup of coffee, emotionally drained after two hours of interrogating burglary suspects. Helen, at the opposite end of the kitchen table, slid forward on her chair, leaned back, and folded her hands in her lap, her face flushed and slightly perspiring. Son Tom, now two and a half years old, was playing beneath the table with an oddball black-and-white kitten. Susan had found it wandering in the alley. It walked sideways like a crab, but otherwise it appeared to be okay.

"This might be the day," Helen said. I looked up at her and before I could respond, a knock came on the kitchen door, and Mavis, the secretary, stepped into the kitchen from the office. This was my sixth year in office; I had two deputies and a secretary now.

"Hi, Helen," Mavis said, then bent down to peer at Tom. "What are you doing under there, Tommy?" she asked.

"Gots a new kitty, he walks funny," Tom said.

"Well, it sure is cute."

"I think we should have it checked over by the vet," Helen said. Mavis nodded, then turned to me.

"Chuck Matson from the Rochester FBI office is here. He'd like to talk to you."

"How many for supper, Mavis?" Helen asked. I glanced at the kitchen clock. It was 3:30.

"Let's see," Mavis responded. "We've got the three burglars; the guy for auto theft ... Irvin Johnson for being drunk and the Cougar for petty theft. That makes six."

I figured Chuck wanted to check on our person charged with auto theft, but I also wanted to finish my coffee and find out more about what Helen meant about this being the day, so I asked Mavis to bring Chuck to the kitchen after about five minutes.

Mavis was back in the office and had closed the door. "Are you having cramps?" I asked Helen.

"Not yet, but I've had a burst of energy today, just like I did before the other kids were born. I've cleaned house upstairs and down and scrubbed all the bedroom floors. I can just kind of tell. We don't have to go to the hospital yet. I'd just like to sit for a while." We were reminiscing about the days when our other children were born when Mavis brought Agent Matson into the room.

"Sit down, Chuck," I said, motioning toward one of the chairs beside the table. "We were just talking about a trip to the maternity ward, but we've got a while yet. What's on your mind? Can I get you some coffee?" Chuck was dressed in a dark suit, white shirt, tie, and black, well-polished shoes. Standard uniform for the FBI. He hesitated before sitting down.

"Sure. I hope I'm not intruding."

"No, that's okay, both Helen and I are a little tired and don't feel like moving. Anything that Helen shouldn't hear?"

"No, I was just in the area . . . a courtesy call more than anything. How's Pete Chiglo at Whalan doing? Have you seen him lately?"

"Not just lately. I see some of the family once in a while. They all have a lot of character. His daughter Pearl works at the courthouse." Helen looked curiously at Agent Matson.

"The FBI aren't after Pete Chiglo, are they?" Helen asked.

Pete and his wife and children lived in Whalan, a little river town of less than a hundred about fourteen miles east of Preston, where they had a combination tavern and grocery. They were also one of the last tobacco growers in the county.

"No," Chuck laughed. "I got acquainted with Pete a number of years ago. We intercepted some correspondence from Russia, where some officials were extorting money from him for protection of his relatives in the Republic of Georgia. At first we were wondering if Pete had Communist ties. He left Georgia when he was a teenager, went to Alaska and prospected for gold, then moved to Canada, and came to the U.S. in 1918. I found out in short order that Pete was no Communist." I noticed Helen wince, and she stood up.

"Excuse me," she said. "I think I'll go upstairs and pack a few things." Helen went upstairs. Chuck looked uncomfortable.

"Relax, Chuck," I said. "I think we've got about a half hour. I take it you rather like Pete."

"Sure do, he's quite a fellow."

"There was a time, I've been told, when a patron of Pete's ran out of money and traded a couple of rabbits for more beer. Two days later the patron came back with money and wanted his rabbits back. 'You no get rabbits,' Pete said, 'kids like rabbits.' And that was the end of it."

Just then Renee and Susan came home from school, stomped the snow from their feet on the rug just inside the front door, scurried through the hallway to the kitchen, and made a beeline for the cookie jar on the counter.

"Hi, Dad," they said without pausing and with nary a look at Chuck; they were used to all kinds of people in the kitchen. The kitty walked a crooked path in their direction.

Chuck looked at Renee, Susan, Tom, and the cat. "I better be going," he said. "Thanks for the coffee . . . and the entertainment." When Chuck left I poured a glass of milk for each of the girls to have with their cookies.

"Where's Mom?" Susan asked.

"She's upstairs getting some of her things together. You'll probably be getting a baby brother or sister today." Without a word they both ran upstairs. I picked up Tom and the kitty and followed. Helen was sitting on the edge of the bed, rather short of breath.

"Renee, will you call Grandma in Chatfield and see if she can come down and stay with you kids?" Helen asked. Renee called from the phone on the shelf in the headboard of the bed.

"Grandpa," Renee said, "is Grandma there? Mom's going to have the baby. Can she stay with us?" There was a long pause while Renee listened, then she handed the phone to Helen. "It's Grandma," she said.

Grandma was at our place within a half hour. Helen had only one other cramp, but from past experience we knew we should be going. We left for Rochester after five, arriving at the hospital about six. It was March 13, 1965, and we were blessed with a fine healthy baby daughter before eight. The next afternoon Renee and Susan accompanied me to the hospital.

"She's got a red face," Susan said as we looked through the glass partition into the nursery. There were four other babies in the room.

Helen was propped up in bed when we came to her room.

"Do you have a name picked out?" Renee asked.

"Jane or Janie," Helen said.

"Oh ish, no," Susan said, and Renee made a face.

"What's wrong with Janie?" Helen said. "I like Jane."

"We looked at her," Renee said. "She's just not a Janie."

"What then?"

"I don't know, but you can't name her Jane," Susan said.

When we left the hospital there was no firm decision on the baby's name. The discussion over the name continued when we got home, and Tom and Grandma joined in. Renee, Susan, and Tom all agreed the baby's name should be Karen. They called Helen at the hospital and all three took turns convincing her.

It was snowing lightly the next morning when Renee, Susan, and I drove to Rochester to pick up Helen and Karen. We were home for about an hour when a knock came on the dumbwaiter from the jail. Renee pulled up a chair to stand on and opened the door. It was Irvin Johnson.

"Ask your mom and dad when I can see the baby. Is it a boy or a girl?" Irvin asked.

"A girl," Renee said. "Her name is Karen. I'll check with Dad and let you know when you can see her."

It was ten o'clock on a Saturday morning, and Tom and I were upstairs in a spare bedroom fixing the tracks for his toy train to a piece of plywood when the phone rang.

"Rod Slowcombe's gone crazy," the caller shouted across the line. "I think he killed his wife, get here right away. Do you know where the farm is?"

"Yes, I've been there before," I said. "I need your name for the report."

"Lawrence Munson," he said.

With Lee Tienter along as special deputy, I drove the nearly thirty miles with a cold nervous feeling in the pit of my stomach. I'd been at Slowcombe's on a domestic call a year or so earlier. By the time I'd got there they'd patched things up, but I still remembered an eerie feeling I had at the time and the peculiar look in Rod Slowcombe's eyes. A speeding ambulance with red lights flashing exited the farm driveway as we approached. The roof of a blazing barn collapsed in a shower of smoke and high-flying embers as we parked by the machine shed, where a dozen frightened men stood huddled together.

"He ran into the house just a little bit ago," one of the men shouted as we alighted from the car. I glanced back at the barn and then back to the men.

"What's the situation?" I asked. "Is Lawrence Munson here?" A tall man with a red cap stepped forward.

"I'm Munson," he said. "I live across the road. Rod stabbed his wife ten or fifteen times with a screwdriver. He ran from the house into the barn when the ambulance came. The ambulance men took her from the house—she was unconscious and all blood. They said there's a big bloody screwdriver on the floor where they picked her up and a rifle on the kitchen table. By then the barn was burning. Rod ran out of it and back into the house just before you drove into the yard."

I saw a fire truck coming about a quarter mile down the road. I didn't welcome the task ahead for Lee and me, but there was no time to ponder. Rod had already stabbed his wife and set fire to the barn, there was a gun in the house—who knew what might happen next? We couldn't wait for him to start shooting. Waiting only gave fear a chance to screw up my thinking process.

"Ready, Lee?" I asked. Lee nodded without any hesitation, and we hurried toward the house. "Take the back, I'll take the front," I said, and Lee ran around the house. There was no way to coordinate our entry. Three wooden steps led up to the front door. I ran up them, opened the door, and stepped into a shabbily furnished kitchen. Rod was seated in one of the kitchen chairs, with a .22 rifle leaning against the table about two feet away. He reached for the gun. I heard Lee burst through the back entryway. "In here, Lee," I said. Rod turned his head toward the back door. Lee stepped into the kitchen. Rod's hand was near the rifle. I was close enough now to rush him if he moved the gun. Rod looked to Lee, then to me, then dropped his hands to his sides.

"I guess I can't take both you bastards out," he said. He looked up at me, a sad pleading look. I approached slowly, picked up the rifle, and handed it to Lee. Rod slumped forward, held his head in his hands, and began to sob.

"I hope I didn't kill her. I would have if the rifle hadn't jammed. I was going to shoot her to death. The screwdriver was in the first drawer I opened. I'd just gone wild. I stabbed and stabbed at her until she lay still. Then I called the neighbor and told him

I'd done it." Then Rod looked up at me with a blank expression and quit talking. By this time Lee had taken the bolt out of the rifle, disabling it.

"The rifle was loaded, Neil," Lee said.

"I got it fixed just before you came in," Rod said.

"We're going to have to take you in, Rod," I said. "You need help." I needed to lock up the house to preserve any evidence at the scene.

"Where's the house key?" I asked Rod. He stared straight ahead and didn't answer. I had Lee look after him while I put the bloody screwdriver in a plastic bag. We found the house keys on a hook on the wall by the telephone.

When Lee and I and Rod stepped outside through the front door, great relief appeared on the faces of the men gathered by the machine shed. We had handcuffed Rod, and Lee ushered him into the back seat and sat beside him. Lawrence Munson motioned me to where he was standing.

"Check with the veterans' service officer," he said. "He's been treated at the vets' hospital before—for a mental condition."

As we took Rod to jail there was a voice in my mind admonishing me. "You stupid ass, you done it again. You dumb SOB, when are you going to learn? You can't keep on taking chances like this. It's not bravery, it's stupidity."

After Rod was locked up, I asked a trusty to keep an eye on him. I then called the county attorney to give him a rundown on what happened, and we continued the investigation. I took Rod to a hearing in probate court on Tuesday, after which I was instructed to take him to the Veterans' Hospital in Tomah, Wisconsin—a federal hospital that specialized in treating veterans' mental disorders. Rod's wife recovered from her multiple stab wounds. Two years later Rod was back on the farm living with his wife.

I changed drastically after this case. I can best describe what came over me by relating a scientific experiment with sheep. The sheep were fitted with a device that gave them mild electric shocks at five-minute intervals, whereupon they would shake for a moment and then continue grazing. Half of the sheep were then fitted with a bell that rang fifteen seconds before the shock. Soon these sheep began to shake when the bell rang and continued to do so until after the shock was received. After about a week the sheep with the bell attached began to die. There was no noticeable detrimental effect to the sheep that were shocked without the warning bell.

The ringing of the telephone became my warning bell. I figured I had been very lucky, unthinkingly dashing into situations like that with Rod. Now for some reason I was scared. I hated to hear the telephone ring and, like the sheep, became edgy, shaking inside, until I found out what the call was about. I knew I wouldn't be running for sheriff again and would be glad when this term in office was over.

When my career in law enforcement began, I held judges, lawyers, and the entire judicial system in the highest esteem. To me, judges were ultimately fair-minded people of unquestionable integrity who attained their position after being recognized as top legal scholars. Lawyers, by their position as officers of the court, I also held in high regard. My respect for some judges and lawyers remains, but my lofty expectations regarding the judicial system began to change significantly as I worked within it.

It was 10:30 A.M. Court had been called for nine, but as usual Judge Turrett was late. Judges would not tolerate others being late in their court, so I, along with a deputy, two men awaiting arraignment on felony charges, and thirty-six prospective jurors, had been waiting since 8:45.

"All rise," the clerk of court directed as Judge Turrett entered the courtroom from chambers. There was a smug look on the judge's face. His mop of long, blue-black hair with ringlets on the back and side matched the color of his judicial robe. His face was rugged, like that of a pro linebacker, and he screened the courtroom with a pair of black eyes set below stiff, bushy eyebrows. I'd worked with Judge Turrett before. To me he appeared arrogant, as if he had been anointed to his position. The prospective jurors appeared impatient and irritated.

Turrett looked down from his lofty perch at the jurors and the rest of us as if we were specks of dust that had settled from the air. He leaned forward, his eyes scanning the jurors, and motioned his hand to the clerk.

"The court clerk here tells me that many of you have asked to be excused from jury duty," he said. "First let me tell you that jury duty in the United States is just that, a duty. A duty to your country, which has granted you citizenship. I will be excusing only those who, for medical reasons, have written statements from a medical doctor. No one, however, for any reason, will be excused today. After adjournment today I want you all to go home and think seriously about your responsibility as citizens, and if you believe you must be excused, come back tomorrow with your written requests and statements from your doctor." He paused and looked at his watch. "The court will be in recess for fifteen minutes. I'll see the county attorney, clerk, and sheriff in chambers," he said.

I was immediately approached by several jurors, including a very irate lady.

"I have an appointment at the Mayo Clinic in the morning. I expected to be excused today," she said.

"You'll have to take your concerns up with the court clerk or the judge," I said. By the time I arrived in chambers, the judge was lining up an afternoon golf game with the clerk.

"See if Probate Judge Stanley could join us," Turrett said to the clerk. "We can have lunch where that good-looking red-haired snatch is the waitress and be on the links by 1:30."

"Sheriff," he said, turning to me, "those men you have for arraignment. Do they have an attorney?"

"No, Your Honor."

"Well, we want to get this over in a hurry. I'll enter pleas of not guilty for them and appoint them an attorney. I expect they're indigent, aren't they?"

"I expect so," I said.

"I see they're both white guys. You never do get any boogies and jungle bunnies down here, do you? You have any in your whole county?"

"You mean Negroes?"

"Yeah."

"We have a quadroon who works at a sawmill over in Rushford," I said.

"Quadroon! What's that?"

"A black person—one-fourth black, that is," I said.

"You're lucky," he said. "Well, let's get back in there and get those boys arraigned."

Before the arraignments the judge dismissed the jurors. "Be back tomorrow at 8:30," he said. An entire day had been wasted for most of them, and two days for those he'd excuse the next day. The arraignments were completed by 11:30.

"The remainder of the calendar will be postponed until tomorrow at 8:30. Court adjourned," announced Judge Turrett.

Several years later I brought before Judge Turrett a man charged with furnishing liquor to minors, his second similar offense—a gross misdemeanor with a maximum penalty of one year in the county jail. Turrett had been an active Democrat before coming to the bench. The defendant's attorney, a former lieutenant governor of Democratic persuasion and a good friend of the judge, made a motion for the case to be heard by the judge without benefit of jury. The county attorney, who never pursued his job with much zeal, didn't object.

We presented a compelling case. Two juveniles positively identified the defendant as the one who sold them the booze. But I wasn't surprised at the judge's ruling.

"I find the defendant not guilty," Judge Turrett pronounced. Then to the defendant standing before him, he said, "Now I know full well you sold this liquor to these kids, and you don't have a license to sell liquor in the first place. And if you ever appear before me in court again I'll throw the book at you." It seemed quite incongruous to me, but by then I was learning.

Judge Andersen was nearly the opposite of Turrett: punctual, scholarly, polite, and deliberate. I respected his work more than any district judge I'd worked with. So it hurt profoundly when I learned that he, too, could succumb to the rites of fraternity.

I had two men before him, fifty-three-year-old Manny Lind and eighteen-year-old Charles Odin. They'd driven too fast across a railroad crossing. At least that's what tripped them up, for they had a three-foot-square safe in their trunk that they'd just stolen from a gas station. As they sped across the crossing on their getaway, the safe bounced out of the trunk onto the highway in front of a following car. Of course the occupants of that car, thinking this rather strange, took down the license number and description of the car and called me. We had the culprits in custody within the hour. After a short interrogation they both fessed up to the burglary and safe job. I further convinced Charles that since this was his first arrest it would be prudent for him to clear his entire record. That way when this was all over he would have a clean slate and wouldn't be continuously looking over his shoulder to the past. He signed confessions to a total of fourteen burglaries, ten of them safe jobs. He'd accompanied Manny on all of them.

Now Manny and Charles faced sentencing on fourteen counts of burglary. This being Charles's first appearance in court, I expected he would get about five years but be released on probation. I had so recommended to the court in the presentence investigation.

Manny's case was something else again. He was a repeat offender who in the late thirties had shot a man in the leg while holding up a gas station. He'd previously served time in prison,

been paroled, and been sent to prison again for further violations—a three-time loser. He'd been up to no good in our area for
some time, but we were never able to catch up with him until now.
I was convinced he would do some time and had so recommended
to the court.

Manny was a gofer, of sorts, for the Krumholtz brothers, two
men who bootlegged liquor during the twenties and thirties and
had a string of slot machines until Governor Youngdahl cracked
down in the forties. After that they were reduced to pinball
machines, punchboards, jukeboxes, and retailing a bit of unli-
censed liquor. They must have been indebted to Manny, and I
expect he knew too much, because they provided him with a good
lawyer, Luther Bang, a past president of the Minnesota State Bar
Association. Charles had a court-appointed attorney, Boyd Hanson. Both Manny and Charles pleaded guilty to the same offenses,
but when it came time for sentencing, Bang, representing Manny,
stepped before the court wearing a white carnation in the lapel of
his five-hundred-dollar pinstriped suit. He appealed for lenience
of the court in sentencing because his client was uneducated and of
low IQ and easily led astray by the likes of his young accomplice.
In each incident he had been drinking and enticed into going
along. If given a chance on probation he would stay away from the
wild youngsters of the community who tended to lead him astray.

"The Krumholtz brothers will guarantee Mr. Lind full and
gainful employment for the entire time of his probation should he
receive it," Attorney Bang concluded.

Hanson, Charles's appointed attorney, farmed as a second
occupation. He appeared before the court in a dark rumpled suit
and high-top work shoes smudged with traces of cow manure. He
made a very short appeal, asking the judge to take into consideration the youth of his client and the fact that he had no previous
record. With the statements complete the judge pondered for a
few minutes, scanning the papers before him.

"Will the defendants please rise," he said, directing his attention to Charles. "Charles Odin, having pleaded guilty to the charge of burglary in the first degree, I hereby sentence you to a maximum term of five years in the Minnesota reformatory at Saint Cloud. You are remanded to the custody of the sheriff to carry out the sentence. You will be given credit for the time you have already served in the county jail."

The judge paused, looked at Manny's presentence report in front of him, and glanced in the direction of Manny and his attorney.

"Manny Lind, having pleaded guilty to the crime of burglary in the first degree, I hereby sentence you to five years in prison at Stillwater, Minnesota. This sentence is suspended under certain conditions of good behavior and you are to be released on probation as soon as you are contacted at the county jail by the state probation officer, who will give you the terms of your probation. Court adjourned."

I couldn't believe it. Not Judge Andersen, no, it just couldn't be!

A few weeks later, while having a drink with the court clerk (a decorated war veteran who during World War II had brought his disabled bomber down in the main street of a Swiss town), I asked his opinion of the Lind decision.

"Judge Andersen was taken aback by his own actions," the clerk said. "He told me he had come to court with the full intention of sentencing both men to prison. He said he'd known Luther Bang for a long time, and before becoming a judge, he, too, was a president of the bar association, and previously they had both served as district officers of the Republican party. He said he didn't know what got into him; it must have been the Christmas season."

For me it was as if I'd completed my finals in Judiciary 101. "It's hard to rule against a fraternity brother."

It didn't do Manny much good, though, because we nailed him on another safe job four months later and his probation was revoked.

In the long run maybe it was for the best for Charles, too. One evening, nearly twenty-five years later, I stopped off at a tavern in Spring Valley, sat down at the bar, and ordered a drink. A tough-looking character from across the bar hollered to the bartender and pointed at me.

"I'll buy that old son-of-a-bitch his drink," he said, loud enough so that everyone in the bar could hear him. I got my drink and the man came over and stood beside me. I wasn't sure who the guy was at first, but I looked him over and it came to me.

"Remember when you took me up to Saint Cloud to prison?" he said.

"Sure do, Charles," I said. Charles was a little drunk and there was a sneer on his face.

"I should whip your ass."

"I should finish my drink first."

"Sounds like a deal to me," Charles said. The sneer had disappeared.

"Who's the woman you're with over there?" I asked. "She looks familiar."

"You know her. She was Moose Cross's wife. You had him up for burglary a few times. He died here a couple of years ago. We're married now."

"Oh, sure. Hi, Evelyn." I waved across the bar to her.

"Hi, Neil," she said. "Haven't seen you for a while." Evelyn came over, and we talked about the old times when Moose was giving us trouble. I ordered a drink for them.

"No way," Charles said. "You were Goddamn good to me when I was in jail, treated me with respect, like we were equal, didn't talk down to me. I'm buying the drinks now, so shut up about it, you old bastard." Evelyn laughed. "You shouldn't talk to

Neil that way," she said. I thought about the time when her former husband, Moose, had infected her with gonorrhea after he had contracted it from a loose seventy-seven-year-old woman in a neighboring town. Doc Nehring and I had quite a time locating all of her lovers in an effort to get the epidemic under control.

"I was really pissed off when I got sent up and Manny didn't," Charles said. "But now I think if I'd've of got off then, I'd been right back at it again. That three years in stir let me grow up a dab. It was tough on me, but I learned my lesson. I never want to go back again." We talked for an hour. I've seen him a couple of times since, and he always calls me an old son-of-a-bitch and won't let me buy any drinks.

Probate and juvenile court was presided over by Judge "Itch" Stanley. The court also handled misdemeanor criminal cases and preliminary hearings on gross misdemeanor and felony charges.

One memorable case before Judge Stanley was the preliminary hearing of a nineteen-year-old, a high school senior, Ralph, who had stolen a car and burglarized a Chatfield grocery store. Floyd Mohawk, the town cop, had a good idea who the guilty party was but wanted me to do the questioning. I contacted the school principal and made a request to see the young man. He decided that since the boy was not a juvenile it would be okay for me to talk to him in his office. I was dressed casually, having made it a practice never to wear a uniform when visiting public schools. The principal brought the boy to his office and stayed in the room with us during the interrogation.

The Miranda court decision, handed down in the mid-sixties, basically says that before officially interrogating a suspect or taking a statement, you must inform the suspect of the following:

1. You have the right to remain silent.
2. Anything you say can and will be used against you in a court of law.

3. You have the right to talk to a lawyer and have this lawyer present with you while you are being questioned.

4. If you cannot afford to hire a lawyer, one will be appointed to represent you before any questioning, if you wish.

5. You can decide at any time to exercise these rights and not answer any questions or make any statements.

6. Do you understand each of these rights I have explained to you?

7. Having these rights in mind, do you wish to talk to us now?

I totally agreed with the Miranda decision. It was needed to prevent rough cops and overzealous police departments from the old-style rubber hose treatment and other illegal tactics. It didn't change our interrogation process, though, because we'd always made it a practice to tell people their rights before questioning them. Now, however, it was more formal. We had cards printed up from which to read people their rights, and we made sure a witness was present who could testify that the rights were read to the suspect. I read Ralph his rights from the card, with the principal as a witness, then gave Ralph the card and had him read it aloud to me.

"Do you fully understand your rights?" I asked.

"Yes," Ralph replied.

"I want to talk to you about a stolen car and a burglary of a grocery store. Are you willing to talk to me about it at this time?"

"Yes."

During a fifteen-minute interview Ralph confessed to stealing the car and burglarizing the store. He told me where the car was hidden and how he'd put some of the loot from the store in a small cave in Chatfield Township. He wrote out a handwritten confession, which he signed. His signature was witnessed by me and the principal. Later in the day I found the stolen car and the loot, just where Ralph indicated it was in the confession. When I brought the information to the county attorney, we thought we had an open-and-shut case.

However, after the Miranda decision it became popular, almost a contest, for judges to find innovative ways to throw out confessions. When this happened, of course, all the evidence obtained as a result of the confession would be suppressed. Judges began falling all over themselves, like a herd of stampeding cattle, to see who could be the most creative in finding reasons to throw out confessions, particularly if one of the defendants' attorneys was influential in the bar association. It became something like a subculture within the judiciary.

When I brought Ralph before Judge Stanley, he ruled the confession was taken under duress because I was larger in physical stature than Ralph and therefore Ralph was fearful of me. All the evidence was suppressed and Ralph took a walk. Itch had a smile for his fraternal brother, the defense attorney.

After that my idealistic views of the judiciary were clouded. I couldn't change my physical stature, so my expertise in interrogation would be of little benefit to the office. Perhaps the county needed a smaller sheriff. I came closer to finalizing my decision to leave law enforcement at the end of my term and began focusing on plans for another vocation I might enter with idyllic innocence and ignorance. The legislature.

Rudy Olafson came to my office imploring me to help him. Rudy was a poor man whose uncle had died six years earlier and left his sister and him nearly four hundred thousand dollars, but Rudy hadn't seen any of the money. The president of an area bank was appointed administrator of the estate and all the money had been tied up in a checking account in his bank for all these years, not even drawing interest. The estate attorney had collected his fee (a percentage of the estate as prescribed by the bar association) but hadn't settled the estate. Rudy and his sister thought the situation was criminal. He asked me to do something about it. I talked to Probate Judge Stanley. He should have been able to expedite matters, but he, the banker, and the estate attorney were social friends.

"Nothing I can do about it," he said.

"But it's just not right," I said.

This was only one of many complaints I received from citizens regarding the handling of estates. Legally there wasn't anything I could do about it. State law provided that estate matters must go through probate court. To proceed before the court you were required to be an attorney. The law provided that probate attorneys were entitled to a percentage of the estate, even without showing services performed. It bothered me a great deal that this chicanery was sanctioned by the courts and the legislature. It was white-collar crime without a penalty. I had a difficult time adjusting to the reality that professionalism doesn't necessarily make people honorable even if they graduate from law school, get a judgeship, put on a black dress, and are elevated to a bench above ordinary citizens, who are commanded to rise when they enter the room.

The main theme of my legislative campaign was probate and other judicial reform.

Mistaken Identity

Molly Poole, a fifteen-year-old sophomore, walked alone on her way home from play practice at the high school. Even though she had been in the new school for only three weeks, having moved to town from a farm in another district, she had been given a part in the one-act play. The moon, mostly obscured by dark clouds, offered little light, and the street lights seemed awfully dim to Molly. She hurried home and felt safer when she closed the front door behind her. She was alone in the house; her widowed mother worked late and wasn't expected home till after midnight. Molly poured herself a glass of milk and watched some of Johnny Carson on TV before going to bed. She quickly fell asleep, leaving the front door unlocked for her mother. When she awoke during the night she assumed the figure sitting on her bed was her mother. By the time her eyes became adjusted to the dim light offered by the street light outside her window, the figure had pulled back the covers and was getting into bed with her. Suddenly she realized the person was a man, and she let out a terrifying scream. The startled man jumped up, grabbed his clothes, and ran from the house. Molly called her mother at work, who in turn called the sheriff's office. When I arrived at their home, Molly was near hysterics and her mother was both frightened and angry. They showed me a pair of brown wing tips, size 12, that the intruder in his haste had left behind.

Sometimes, in small towns, a person can know way too much about people. For a sheriff, though, often this can come in handy.

"Do you think the man was drinking, Molly?" I asked. "Could you smell liquor?"

"I think so," she replied.

I calmed the mother and daughter down and told them not to worry. I was pretty sure this was just a case of mistaken identity. I told them that the lady who lived in the house previously had an occasional visitor who took a drink now and again. I thought perhaps after imbibing he may have forgotten that the lady had moved to another house.

"I'm pretty sure I know where to take the shoes," I said. "And I'm positive there is nothing to worry about, but I'll get back to you."

I took the wing tips with me and a couple of days later pulled up to the gas pumps outside Charlie Benson's country store near Wykoff. Charlie was known to take a drink or two from time to time. There wasn't self-service in those days; Charlie came out to pump the gas.

"Five dollars' worth, Charlie," I said. "Nice day."

Charlie looked a little sheepish while he pumped the gas and cleaned the windshield. When he was through I looked in my billfold.

"I'm a little short of cash today, Charlie," I said. "Could I charge it?"

"Sure," he said. I got out of the car and went to the trunk.

"Maybe you should have some collateral, Charlie," I said. I opened the trunk door and brought out the shoes. Charlie turned seven colors of red and shook his head.

"You sum-bitch, Neil," he muttered.

I handed Charlie the shoes and a five-dollar bill and was on my way.

Kidnapped

Joseph Parks, sweating profusely, fought against the ropes that trussed him to the chair. His wrists were worn raw, and the sweat running into his eyes was nearly blinding. More than a half hour had passed since the two men had taken his car, credit cards, identification, billfold, and money and tied him to the chair. It was July 22, 1959. The air was stale, hot, humid, and laced with a rank musty manure odor. Looking about, he surmised that he was in an old chicken coop; the dirt-caked windows were tightly closed and the unpainted pine door was firmly closed. Joseph took several deep breaths to calm his nerves. He'd begged the men not to kill him but if they were going to, to "please pull the trigger and make it quick."

Now he began to wonder how he would die. Heart failure would be the quickest and least painful, he thought. He'd suffered a mild heart attack four years ago and had high blood pressure. Further stress and panic without his medication would surely bring the end. Otherwise he'd dehydrate quickly in this heat and suffer a slow, torturous death.

Gilbert La Fountaine and Granrud Olafson escaped from a Marine Corps brig in Oceanside, California, where they were being held for armed robbery; they stole a car and made their way east. Olafson, originally from Minnesota and the nephew of a former governor, laid out the route. During four days on the road they stole a second car in Minneapolis. Near Preston, Minnesota, they pulled off the highway onto an unused driveway, which led them through a thick grove of hardwood trees to an old shack in a small clearing. They stepped out of the car, stretched, and walked about the clearing, planning their next move. Short on money and gas, they decided to wait until after dark to pull a holdup unless opportunity presented itself sooner.

That same afternoon, at 3:15, Joseph Parks, a Skelly Oil district representative, parked his car, taking advantage of the shade of three oak trees located near the wide shoulder of Highway 52, two miles north of Preston. Oppressed by the heat of the day, he rolled his window down and opened the passenger door to allow what little breeze there was to cool his brow. He removed his necktie, untied his shoes, stretched, and then became engrossed in organizing the paperwork he'd neglected at his last three business calls.

"Move over, Pop," a gruff voice demanded. Something hard was pressed against his left temple. Joseph turned and found himself looking into the barrel of a handgun, held by a raw-boned, tough-looking young man with several days' growth of dark beard. Joseph moved to the right side of the seat as commanded; the gun looked like a .38 police revolver.

"Now sit still and be quiet," the gunman said. Another young man, taller, somewhat over six feet, appeared from behind the car and entered the back seat.

"Let's get a move on," he said.

"Okay, let's go back to the clearing we just came from. You follow in the other car. The old gent can ride with me," the gunman said.

Joseph remained quiet, as ordered, but his mind panicked and his heartbeat raced. He was nearing retirement, looking forward to spending time at the cabin he and his wife had recently purchased on Cross Lake. "Now," he thought, "it will be all over." He'd be on his last ride, to who knows where.

When they arrived at the clearing, the taller man, having followed in the second car, ushered Joseph out of the car and ordered him to raise his hands and fold them above his head. The shorter man held him at gunpoint while the other went through his pockets, taking the contents and turning each pocket inside out when he was through.

"What are we going to do with him now?" the shorter man said, after taking all of Joseph's belongings.

"Take him over to the shack," the other replied.

Joseph noticed the weeds and grass on the way to the shack were tall and green. The vegetation on the pathway wasn't even wilted; evidently no one had been back here for months. The robbers hardly spoke, but the furtive looks they gave each other when glancing toward him sent shivers through Joseph's spine. The man with the gun motioned him inside the shack. For some strange reason Joseph noticed the second man had very large hands and feet.

"Let's tie him to the chair," the gunman said. They bound him securely with a rope from a fence stretcher that was hanging on a nail by one of the dirty windows, then departed without a word. Joseph soon heard the two cars drive away.

Forty-five minutes later, Joseph, desperate in his effort to free himself, had nearly given up, when it came to his mind that he had untied his shoes when he had stopped by the highway. His feet were tied securely to the inside legs of the chair but a glimmer of hope came when, after several more minutes, he was able to work his right shoe off. Shortly thereafter he manipulated his heel above a strand of rope. Slack in the rope allowed his foot to come loose. It took only another few minutes for Joseph to free himself and dash outside into the deserted clearing, where he gulped fresh air into his lungs.

I received the call at the sheriff's office at 5:00 P.M. An area farmer had been hailed down on the highway by an older man wearing a suit—a highly unusual sight in Fillmore County. I drove to the farmer's house where Joseph was waiting, listened to his story, and arranged for medical attention.

Two days later, we found his car in a neighboring county, shoved over a steep wooded embankment and wiped clean of fingerprints. We found a credit card customer receipt lodged under the seat, signed by Joseph Park, only Joseph had been spelled Joeseph. This became a vital key to our investigation.

Over a year later we were notified that Olafson was being held in a federal prison in Tulsa, Oklahoma, for interstate transportation of a stolen vehicle. He confessed to the robbery and kidnapping in Fillmore County. Further investigation revealed his escape with La Fountaine. From an array of mug shots Joseph Parks identified both suspects as the men who had abducted him.

Olafson was returned to Minnesota in March 1962. Only nineteen years old at the time, he had a long history of criminal behavior as a juvenile. After pleading guilty to charges of kidnapping and armed robbery, he was sentenced to a term of up to fifteen years in the Saint Cloud State Reformatory.

In the summer of 1962 Gilbert La Fountaine was located in Florida, where he worked as a firefighter, and he was brought to Preston for trial. The city officials where he worked were shocked at the revelation, as was his wife, who knew nothing of his past. The pre-sentence investigation revealed that his firefighter evaluations were of the highest standards, he was punctual, and he had no record of absenteeism. Every member of the fire department spoke highly of him. While in jail, he seemed contrite and resigned to his prospect of serving a long term in prison. I began thinking that, at twenty-nine, maybe he'd outgrown his wild stage during the previous three years. He certainly lived as a reformed person. His wife, along with their baby daughter and his mother, from

Toledo, Ohio, came to visit him at the jail while he awaited sentencing. They were very gracious people. I still have a card of congratulations that Gilbert's mother sent to us when our son Tom was born.

Before Gilbert entered a plea, the county attorney, Gilbert's appointed counsel, and I met and discussed a reduced charge of robbery that carried a maximum term of five years. I had many gut-wrenching, emotional misgivings about the arraignment that I kept to myself. All I had to do was speak up and the county attorney would have continued with the original charges of armed robbery and kidnapping, resulting in a fifteen-year sentence.

La Fountaine pleaded guilty to the reduced charge of robbery, for which he was sentenced to from zero to five years at the prison in Stillwater. The kidnapping charge was dropped.

I spent many a sleepless night before and after I made a favorable recommendation to the court. Some type of intuition told me that Gilbert deserved another chance, and I so recommended to the court. Later, I occasionally got sick to my stomach thinking of how I'd feel if I had been wrong about this man and something terrible happened. Six months later he was released on parole, and my anxiety increased. About once a year over the next thirty-four years my mind continued to pester me about La Fountaine until August 1, 1997, when, through the marvel of the Internet, I found a telephone number in Florida for Gilbert La Fountaine and gave the number a call. A man answered on the second ring.

"Is this Gilbert La Fountaine?" I asked.

"Yes."

"I'm Neil Haugerud. I used to be sheriff in Fillmore County, Minnesota. Do you remember me?" There was a long pause.

"Yes, I sure do."

"Gilbert, I've been kind of bothered all these years, wondering how you turned out after your release from Stillwater." Another long pause.

"Damn, Neil, it's good to hear from you. I've never even had a traffic ticket since I got out. How the hell did you find me? Oh, that's right, you found me before, too, didn't you?"

"I'm real glad to hear that, Gilbert. You still a fireman?"

"No, I got fired when I was in prison and they didn't hire me back. I got other work, though, and I'm retired now. How's your wife and family?"

"Fine, Gilbert, fine. I'm writing some stories about when I was sheriff. I was wondering if you might send me a letter letting me know what you thought about your experience here in Minnesota."

"Be more than glad to, Neil. I've taken up a bit of writing myself; I'll send some of it along."

Gilbert and I talked on for another fifteen minutes.

On August 15, 1997, I received a personal letter, along with several of Gilbert's writings, one of which he won an award for in the 1997 annual News-Press Fish Tales contest. Following are excerpts from Gilbert's letter.

Dear Neil & Family,

I'm sending a little material and a few pictures to show what it's like to be 65 years old and retired.

When I think back, it seems like it was last week, when you picked me up in Pensacola. I was actually glad it was all over, I was tired of running. But my biggest fear was the time I would have to serve. Especially with a wife and child.

At that point, I felt I had in a small way rehabilitated myself by being straight and being on the fire department. I never did like trouble. Just one of those bad times in my life that I knew I would have to pay for eventually. When we arrived in Preston I didn't know what to expect.

I later realized the importance of where it starts. The way you are treated in jail before you are sentenced. I thank you and your deputies for the way you treated me.

Also your wife for all the good food, especially on Thanksgiving and Christmas.

Once I was sentenced to 0 to 5 years I knew I still had a good life ahead of me. I always thought you had something to do with that, too. Thank you.

Once I got to Stillwater I made up my mind to take advantage of all or any courses that were offered plus work in the factory. I went up for parole after six months and received it. Unbelievable, but it was true. I learned a lot in prison, that's why I have written about it. I hope you can use some of this. You can keep everything, and you have my permission to use any of it.

I wish you the best on your writing endeavors.

Yours,
Gil

I would like to share with the readers several things that have taken place since Helen and I left the jailhouse at the end of 1966. Regrettably, Dr. Nehring died in January 1967, after a strenuous effort to resuscitate a child who drowned. A marble monument placed outside the city hall in Preston is dedicated to Dr. Nehring. The plaque is inscribed as follows.

IN MEMORY OF JESSE POTTER NEHRING,
WHO PRACTICED MEDICINE IN THIS AREA
FROM AUGUST 10TH, 1930, UNTIL JANUARY 25TH, 1967.
HIS DEVOTED SERVICE TO HIS PATIENTS AND HIS NOTABLE CONTRIBUTION
TO THE CARE OF THE SICK AND TO THIS COMMUNITY
WILL BE FOREVER REMEMBERED.

This plaque is placed here by the residents of Preston and surrounding area.

Doctor Nehring was one of my favorites, an expert at deflating pretension and a fine friend who loved his wife and family dearly. I should have mentioned in the body of the book that June 21, 1964, was proclaimed Dr. Nehring Day for Preston and the surrounding community. Hundreds from the community honored Doc at an open house in the auditorium of the Preston High School. During his career in the Preston area he delivered nearly six thousand babies without a single maternal death.

My book portrays a Doc Nehring most of his patients and many in the community didn't have the opportunity to meet. I think they missed a unique slice of life. He looked the part of a typical country doctor, a bit on the portly side, five foot ten, with light brown thinning hair. His facial features were round and cherubic; an almost childlike face with grapelike eyes and downy cheeks, and he had a trailing voice that could lead you beyond the edge of an imaginary cliff and drop you off like a character in the comics. He is sorely missed.

In June 1996, when I first began writing these stories, I attended a week-long creative nonfiction writing workshop at the University of Iowa in Iowa City. My homework for the third day was to write about something I observed after class. I was, however, about to learn more about modern policing than about writing.

Being ever aware of my surroundings, I attended a 9:00 P.M. authors' reading at the auditorium. Afterward, on my way to my hotel, I stopped at a sports bar and had a cheeseburger and fries while sipping two glasses of white wine during the remainder of the Bulls-Sonics game on TV. It was my first half day without a removable cast on my lower leg. Having previously injured my Achilles tendon, I limped on toward my hotel, taking my time, observing late-night activities on the pedestrian mall. There were red benches in the mall so I sat for a while to take notice. A dark-skinned young man playing a guitar sang in a doorway, a teenager played a game with two wool-tipped sticks, and men in their twenties shouted upward from the street and laughed in response to a woman's flirtatious voice from an upper story. Two police officers were fussing with a ragged man on another bench, and I shuffled near to observe and gather material for class. The larger of the two gentry stepped in my direction and kind of stood in my face.

"Can I help you?" he asked. His manner was more threatening than helpful.

"No," I said. "I'm just observing."

"Move along," he commanded, thrusting his jaw inches from my face.

"I think I'll just watch," I said, and folded my arms across my chest—another mistake.

"Move along or you will be under arrest for interfering with an officer."

It would have been easier and probably smarter on my part to just move along. But I'd perceived changes in police attitudes since I was sheriff in Minnesota in the sixties, and Andy of Mayberry this officer wasn't. I wanted to learn from experience whether some police could be as arrogant as I'd heard. I decided to stand firm—to stand up for my constitutional rights.

"What specifically am I doing to interfere, Officer?" I asked. He didn't appreciate my inquiry.

"Have you been drinking?" he asked.

"A couple glasses of wine," I answered.

"You're under arrest for public intoxication," he responded.

"What reasons do you have to consider me intoxicated?" I asked.

"We saw you walking down the street. You were unsteady."

"I'm not intoxicated and believe I have a constitutional right to continue in this public place," I said.

"Hands behind your back," growled the irate keeper of the peace. The other gendarme came over to assist. I thought this pair could be dangerous, and a stab of fear warned me of possible consequences should I question their authority. I was handcuffed, my hands behind my back, and I was very polite and quiet as I was hauled off to the hoosegow.

As the first rays of the morning sun seeped between the bars on the window, I looked to the clock on the nightstand for the time. No clock this morning, no nightstand either. In my drowsiness I hadn't yet acclimated myself to my surroundings. I'd slept the night in an orange jumpsuit, on a lower bunk with a stiff plastic-covered mattress and a ragged gray blanket for a pillow.

I stood up and peered out the narrow head-high window. The lattice work bars cast an evil shadow across the bunk. If I'd had pencil and paper I'd have jotted down my observations for class.

Pain in my Achilles tendon reminded me to stand only on my left leg as I hopped over to a stainless steel sink with matching toilet bowl, pushed a silvery button, and, lacking a drinking cup, sucked a drink of water from cupped hands beneath a stubby faucet.

Thinking maybe the innkeepers would have some aspirin, I knocked forcefully on my blue steel bedroom door. During my days as an innkeeper in Minnesota, we always had coffee and sweet rolls for our guests about 7:00 A.M. No one responded to my knock so I rapped again, without success. Some time later (it must have been more than an hour) I heard an electronic click unlocking the door mechanism and from somewhere in the steel-walled corridors my name echoed off the walls.

"Haugerud, get over here. It's eight o'clock. You're going to court," a curt voice commanded.

"I have an injured Achilles and shouldn't walk barefoot on cement floors. I'll need my cast from the hotel room or crutches," I replied in a loud voice. My doctor had said that if they'd have to operate it could be as much as a year for me to recover.

"Hobble over here," the angry voice from somewhere out of sight demanded.

"No," I said pleasantly. I expect it's difficult for me to learn. Was my memory void of what had happened the previous night when I'd said no to an Iowa City officer's command? The officers decided to administer a little more discipline. One of them poked his head into my doorway.

"You can walk or hobble over here like we say and do it now! Or we lock you up until you're thinking straight." The guy's attitude kind of pissed me off.

"I'm not moving without my cast, crutches, or a wheelchair," I said.

"We don't do stuff like that," the innkeeper growled. The door slammed shut, and they kept me incommunicado a while longer.

Sitting on the bunk I recalled the Sunday morning long ago when I responded to a knock from inside my jail when I was sheriff.

"Sheriff, I've got to check my trap line. Sometimes farm dogs get caught in my traps." It was Joe Drury. I'd incarcerated Joe the previous evening for his part in a barroom brawl.

Then Charlie McMurphy called from the back bull pen. He'd gotten drunk the previous afternoon and had not made it home for chores. He pleaded with me to let him out to milk his cows. I figured Joe and Charlie weren't bad guys, so I took Charlie out to his farm and left him off to milk his cows while Joe and I checked the trapline. Sure enough, we found a black farm dog caught in a trap. Joe and I found a cedar post and forced the trap open from a distance. We finished checking the line, and by the time we drove back to Charlie's farm he was through milking. I had Charlie and Joe back in jail before lunchtime. But that was long ago.

Now it was well past noon. I still didn't have my coffee and sweet roll, or my cast from the hotel. The gendarme paid me another visit.

"Had enough and ready to go to court?" he asked.

"Would you at least bring my shoes?" I pleaded. Reluctantly he brought me my shoes. I thought I might be offered a towel, a washcloth, and my comb before being hustled off to court. I was mistaken. As if I were a desperado from the Wild West, two officers drove me to the courthouse.

The tight-lipped, dark-haired Iowa judge couldn't muster a smile as I limped before her bench in my orange jumpsuit, my gray thinning hair as unruly as Grandpa Munster's. After pleading not guilty I promised to return for trial and was released. I was later found not guilty of public intoxication.

The next afternoon, after completing my writing workshop, my 1979 Ford pickup, "Old Rusty," and I headed north on the interstate. An hour into our journey we were confronted by a horde of officers directing all traffic off our side of the highway. I parked as directed by an officer in a Smoky Bear hat.

"Vehicle safety check," he said. "May I see your driver's license?"

I was tempted to say, "If this is a vehicle safety check, why do you need my driver's license?" But I didn't want to put Rusty in jeopardy. So I gave the officer my license and he began the safety check. The headlights worked—high beam, low beam—and the turn signals in front and rear were fine. Taillights fine. Brake lights?

"Push on your brakes again," said the officer; then he came to my open window and began writing.

"Brake lights work?" I asked.

"Yes, but the right light seems brighter than the left. I'm issuing a ticket for faulty equipment."

"But both brake lights are in proper working order?"

"We have candle power requirements, sir," the trooper replied, in a coarse sandpaper voice he must have learned at state patrol school, and handed me the ticket.

"Good thing you can't talk, Rusty," I said in the quiet part of my mind, "or we'd both find our asses locked up again."

Several hours later I crossed over into Minnesota bluff country near where I live. I began to observe the everyday things in my surroundings. I saw rows of middle-aged pine trees touching, as if holding hands, in windbreaks, and ash trees wearing leaves like green prom dresses, and road ditches abounding in dandelions, their white coiffures waiting for the romance of the wind. And in the hills, I was welcomed by a clear-water wink of a trout stream winding its way across the valley floor. Narrow township roads, tunneled and canopied by roadside trees, guided me through rickety one-lane bridges bringing me ever closer to home. Deep in the Root River Valley, a ten-degree drop in the temperature and the sundown mist rising on the black-green hills brought on a pleasant feeling of nostalgic loneliness. And finally the silo on my farm, like an exclamation point on the horizon, told me I was home.

"I never thought I'd be going to bed with a jailbird," my wife of forty-two years said before we drifted off to sleep, safe in the comfort of our country house, five miles from town and far from Iowa City.

Less than two weeks later, three Iowa City police officers, after noticing a door slightly ajar late at night, became suspicious and entered a business. One of them, seeing a young man talking on the telephone, shot and killed him. It was the owner of the business, who frequently worked at night. The lights were on and the place was well illuminated. The case was profiled on national television. The policeman said he thought the man was a burglar. The official position of the police department and the district attorney was that the officers did nothing wrong, and they prevailed. I'm wondering when it became legal for police officers to shoot suspected burglars.

Recently, after a meeting in Minneapolis, I had a more gratifying experience. I'd driven 140 miles and was nearly home. At 6:30 P.M. I stopped to have a sandwich at the Twelve Point Grille in Fountain. There were no other patrons in the establishment and only one waitress, a diminutive, lively young brunette with large hoop earrings. I sat down at the bar.

"Not much action here," I said.

The waitress slid a cardboard Grain Belt coaster in front of me, ignoring my comment.

"What'll you have?" she asked pleasantly enough. "You want a menu?"

"I'll have a pork tenderloin sandwich and coffee while I wait," I replied. She hustled off to the kitchen with my order, then cruised back with my coffee. Having lived in the area my entire life I tend to assume I should know most people. If I don't I'm not bashful about speaking up.

"I'm not sure we've met before," I said.

"Maggie Shores," she said.

"Shores," I said. "That's not a familiar name to me."

"It's my married name. My dad's from this area. Kent Fraser, maybe you know of him." I looked away and chuckled to myself. I'd been checking about, trying to find the whereabouts of Kent Fraser for several months now without success. I was wondering how he might have survived the past thirty-some years. Then I thought maybe Maggie's dad was a different Kent Fraser.

"I used to know a Kent Fraser," I said. And without thinking, I asked in a humorous tone, "Did your dad ever do any time?" As soon as I'd said it, I wished I hadn't. Maggie was washing some glasses in the sink. She looked up at me and laughed.

"Certainly not," she said. "Who in the world are you, anyway?"

"Oh, I'm sorry—Neil Haugerud," I said. "I live near Carimona." Her face lit up.

"You're the guy who writes those jailhouse stories in the paper, aren't you?"

"That's me," I replied.

"I just love those stories," she responded with an open-mouthed smile. I noticed her tongue was pierced—it looked like she had an emerald on her tongue. She dried her hands with a towel, then leaned on the bar in front of me, a puzzled look on her face.

"You know," she said quizzically, "we were talking about those stories one time and Dad said he was in a couple of them. You don't use real names, do you?"

"Mostly not," I said.

"Well, we just laughed and said, 'Ya, right, Dad.' And he just looked amused and didn't say any more."

"Tell me a little about your dad," I said.

"There's five of us girls. I'm the youngest. We think the world of Dad; he's baby-sitting at my place right now, till I get off from work. He's worked for a manufacturer in Rochester for about thirty years." Maggie waited for my response. I decided I'd be better off leaving well enough alone. Luckily a bell rang from the kitchen and Maggie went to get my order. When she came back I hurriedly picked up my sandwich and began eating.

"More than likely a different guy, Maggie," I said, and looked toward the door to the street.

"Oh no, you don't, Neil," she said. "You're not getting off that easy. You might as well tell me now or I'll be grilling Dad anyway."

"Tell you what I'll do," I said. "I saw an old group picture from my sheriff days not long ago. I'll go get it and be right back. I live only five miles from here." I took the rest of my sandwich and told Maggie to save my drink. I was gone about fifteen minutes. I showed Maggie the picture, which was taken in 1961. Four young men were sitting with me in the sheriff's office, wearing white jail-house coveralls.

"Recognize anyone?" I asked Maggie, whose eyes widened like a night owl in a hayloft. She put her forefinger on one of the men in the picture.

"This one smoking the cigarette; that's my Dad," she said. I began wondering what kind of useless trouble I might have gotten myself and Kent Fraser into. Maggie looked away and wiped nervously at the counter where there was nothing to wipe. Her complexion turned a dusty white and her lower lip quivered.

"It can't be—Dad never mentioned anything—I—we had no idea. Was he in prison?" I tried to find a way to dodge the question.

"Let's put it this way," I said. "I had him in jail a few times when I was sheriff. Check and see if your dad wants to tell you anything more. When you talk to him tell him I'd like to sit down with him sometime and talk over old times. Tell him I'm very proud of him."

"We all are, too," Maggie said.

About three weeks later, while having coffee in a Preston business place, a person I thought I should know but didn't recognize approached me.

"Hey, Neil, you old so-and-so. How you doin'?" he said. I looked at him for what seemed a long time while he just stood and smiled.

"Kent Fraser?" I finally asked.

"Sure is," he responded.

"Well, I'll be damned; you're looking good," I said. Kent's looks had changed significantly even though he'd retained the roundness of his features. There was the familiar glint in his eyes and that inescapable sly smile that made him recognizable to me. "Got time for lunch, Kent?" I asked. "I'll buy."

"Sure, let's go to the drive-in. I'm kind of particular about what I eat. We can sit inside," he said.

The drive-in was a small, quiet place. We ordered our lunch and sat down.

"I hope I didn't get you in trouble when I met your daughter Maggie," I said. Kent just shrugged and let his eyes say things were okay, two mannerisms I remembered.

"No, I got good kids," he said.

"This is the first I've seen you since I took you to the Saint Cloud reformatory. How long were you there?"

"A little over three years," Kent said. "You heard about when my brother Lyle drowned, didn't you?"

"No," I said.

"He did two hitches in Vietnam. Came back pretty messed up—a steel plate in his head and screwed up on drugs and booze. He was out fishing in the river; drowned in about six inches of water, pretty strange I'd say. Remember, Lyle was the one Helen fed the baby food to. God, that was funny." In my mind I pictured those two little boys the first time they got in trouble when they were about eleven years old.

"Very sorry to hear about Lyle," I said. "How about you? You must have straightened right out at some point. Your daughter Maggie sure thinks the world of you." Kent shifted in his seat, his chest puffed, and a look of satisfaction came to his face.

"My wife had a lot to do with that," he said. "It was shortly after our first baby was born. I was drinking pretty heavy then. One day my wife just up and says, 'Kent, I've decided something. You have to make up your mind: is it going to be the booze or the family? It's up to you—your choice.' She wasn't mad or anything, just stated it as a fact; she'd made up her mind and I knew it. I chose the family and haven't had a drink since."

Kent and I sat and talked for more than an hour. He told me all about his family and how proud he was of them and his work record. During our conversation Kent brought up the names of at least eight other guys who had been in the Fillmore jail for everything from burglary to bum checks. They too were all leading productive lives as good citizens. "Some of us just get on a rocky path for a while and take a little longer growing up," he said.

When we finished talking, I told him I'd like to include our story in my book.

"Okay," he said, "but don't use my real name; use the name you used in the stories that were in the paper."

I'd had a good day and things seemed right with the world.

Neil Haugerud began his career in public office when he was elected sheriff of Fillmore County in 1958. In 1968, he was elected to the Minnesota House of Representatives, where he served until 1977. He was appointed chairman of the Upper Mississippi River Basin Commission by President Carter in 1977. He began publishing the column "Jailhouse Stories" in the *Fillmore County Journal* in 1997, and now lives in rural Preston, Minnesota, with his wife, Helen. They have three grown daughters (their son, Tom, died at age 15) and three grandchildren.